AF506211

Lessons from the Pandemic:

Ten Touchstones on the Road to Recovery

by Brian Bard

Copyright 2023 © Brian Bard

All rights reserved. No part of this publication may be reproduced, translated, stored in a retrieval system, or transmitted by any means – electronic, mechanical, photocopying, recording, or otherwise – without the prior written consent of the author, except by a reviewer, who may quote brief passages in a review.

To access the free ebook, visit invitedinvocation.com or one of our publishing partners listed there.

The material in this book is for educational purposes and does not replace diagnosis or treatment by a qualified mental health professional. The author cannot guarantee any results expressed or implied herein, and cannot be liable for any outcomes pertaining to users of this book's content.

Cover images credited under Works Cited

ABOUT INVOCATION SPIRITUAL GUIDANCE 

I'm Brian Bard, a Spiritual Guide, Director, and Coach with services in Minneapolis, St. Paul, the greater Twin Cities MN area, and online. I'm also a writer with a series of novels in the works, and am active on the InVocation blog exploring spirituality, social issues, and mythology.

I've facilitated workshops, classes, ceremonies, and retreats in many different settings: community organizing/activism, funerals, memorials, grief support groups, spiritual communities, schools, theater, and universities. And since 2020, I've had countless conversations with people about their experiences during the Pandemic Era, and what they're hoping for from the Recovery Era. I've drawn from all these experiences to assemble these Lessons from the Pandemic, as well as upcoming, comprehensive courses on processing grief and finding your calling. I'm always available to for events speaking engagements, on these topics and more!

Beyond these, I offer guidance for individuals, couples, families, and groups of all beliefs, bodies, and backgrounds in a wide variety of spiritual matters. I accompany and coach clients as they connect with Spirit, Soul, and the Sacred, offering steady presence and fresh insight. Head to my website – invitedinvocation.com – to learn more about my services, my background and training, and a free consult.

I hope to keep working with you in some capacity, and to count you as a subscriber to the InVocation blog!

GRATITUDES 

Welcome to this conversation on our Lessons from the Pandemic – thank you so much for being part of it! I sincerely hope you, your loved ones, and your community find this book helpful in the transition to the Recovery Era.

I want to thank those who made this guidebook possible: Ned Abenroth, Nicole Greenwald, Mary Kietzmann, Katie Kreitzer, Scott McRae, Kyle Petricek, Ellie Roscher, Paul Stoltenberg, Peter Watkins, Kirk Webb, Ellen Weber for their wise counsel; John & Leslie Williams for their gracious hospitality; Marsha Arndt & Rick Nelson, Jill & Chris Bishop, Nick Dailey-Arndt, Margot Dailey, Perrine Dailey, and the Illuman community for their love and support; Jordan Bishop for her brilliant filmography; and Devin Bard, as always, for everything.

I also want to acknowledge that I reside and work on the ancestral homelands of resilient indigenous peoples: the Dakota Sioux, Lakota Sioux, and Anishinaabe Ojibwe First Nations. I offer my gratitude to them for their historical and continued stewardship of this place, for their care and wisdom. And I offer my gratitude to the land itself for the gift of life, for its care and wisdom. Wherever we live, may all of us work for a future where our local Nations and their lands are thriving.

And, outside of just this book, may all of us also continue working to heal the world in the wake of the COVID-19 Pandemic. May we live in ongoing solidarity alongside those with fewer resources, at home and abroad, so they too can begin moving toward recovery.

Brian Bard
InVocation Spiritual Guidance
Minneapolis, MN, USA

CONTENTS 

LESSONS FROM THE PANDEMIC

Ten Touchstones on the Road to Recovery

If you feel inspired, you can send me a tip or support my work:

Every dollar you contribute enables me to offer
free and affordable spiritual guidance during a difficult time for our world.
Thank you for considering!

TOUCHSTONE 1
STORYTELLING

TOUCHSTONE 2
BEING IN NATURE

TOUCHSTONE 3
CREATIVE PROJECTS

TOUCHSTONE 4
EULOGIZING

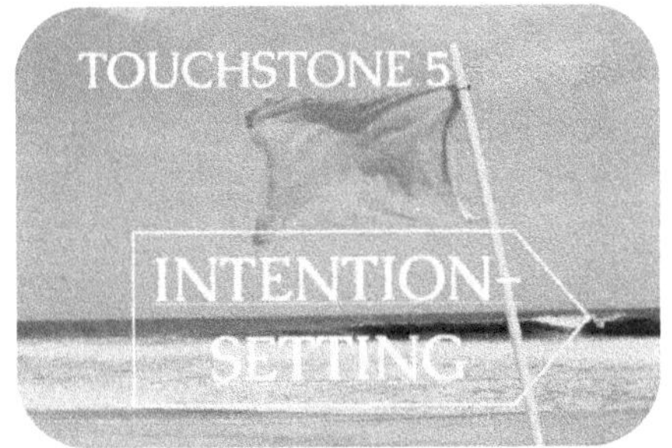
TOUCHSTONE 5
INTENTION-SETTING

TOUCHSTONE 6
SACRED TIMES

TOUCHSTONE 7
SACRED PLACES

TOUCHSTONE 8
RADICAL PRESENCE

TOUCHSTONE 9
VILLAGE LIFE

TOUCHSTONE 10
THE MARGINS

INTRODUCTION

<u>The Roadmap to Recovery</u>

> ➤ What lessons have *you* personally learned from the COVID-19 Pandemic Era?
>
> ➤ What have we learned as a global human family, and what do we need to learn?
>
> ➤ Why is it important?
>
> ➤ What do we do about it?

These are big, daunting questions. But I'm convinced we need to be asking them right now, before the pandemic fades completely into the background of our experience.

In this book, I'll first illuminate why holding these questions in focus is absolutely essential to our post-pandemic transition and growth going forward. Then I'll share some concrete actions we can all take, as individuals and collectively, in our personal, professional, and social lives. These insights draw on many observations, conversations, and research I've been doing as part of InVocation Spiritual Guidance's community pandemic recovery work.

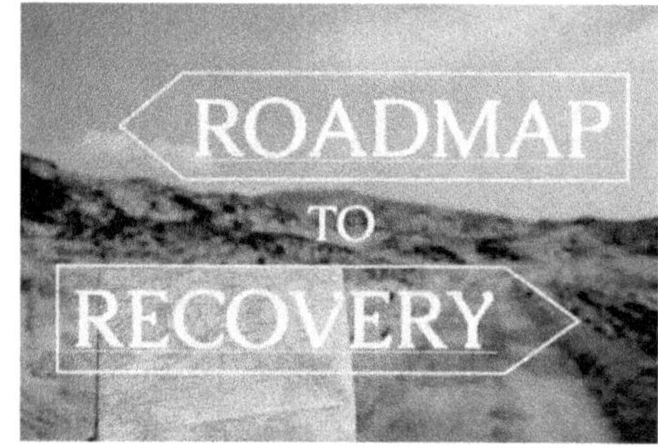

<u>Why is this important?</u>

I expect for some folks at this stage, the third question above may stand out. For many of us, by the time we passed two years since the pandemic began, it had mostly ebbed from our awareness. Why is this conversation still important? Why should we care? Haven't we had enough of pandemic-talk? The world keeps turning, life goes on – why shouldn't we?

Out of everything we've endured in the Pandemic Era, I think *passion* – in a word – is what we've been most deprived of. That vitality, vivacity, vigor, and verve – that's what we most need to reclaim. But it's still eluding us.

The hardship of these past few years has worn a lot of us out. Maybe you've felt it. There's a malaise and melancholy that still afflicts many of us, a slump and stupor, a sort of social hangover you can sense when you talk to people or show up in community spaces. Students, employees, and eventgoers are less engaged than they were before the pandemic. People are less active and energized in their relationships and their private lives. There's less excitement and zest for life than before 2020. We're more disoriented, distracted, and disconnected.[1,2,3,4]

Even if you haven't felt it palpably yourself, the data, as we'll cover in this book, show it plain as day: We're in a kind of *collective long-COVID*. And we need to shake out of it. We're still living in a hazy grogginess, and we need to wake up.

We need to get back to the passion we once knew. We need to rebound and recover. And we may even have the chance to usher in a new era beyond the Pandemic Era – a Passionate Era. But unfortunately, we can't teleport to that destination. We have a journey ahead of us.

In the three years of the Pandemic Era, we've experienced a worldwide communal trauma. And when we look at the history of similar mass traumas – or even personal traumas – there is a clear common message: merely moving *on* is not possible – only moving *through* is.

In other words, we have to proactively process what we've been through, or it will haunt and soon sabotage us. We have grieving to do, and grieving denied is only grieving deferred and intensified. We have to talk about what we've been through, and what the future holds. Some of us only have a little grief to process from these past few years, some of us have a lot – everyone has some, even if it's not apparent. And rather than pretending we can bypass it, we need to move through it to find our way back to passion.

Furthermore, the pandemic has provided us with a planetary-scale natural experiment in how to – and how not to – deal with suffering and grief. These are fixtures of the human experience, and we should be eager to learn how to handle them more skillfully, especially since our modern culture is so ill-equipped and hasn't yet learned from the mistakes of the past. If we don't review and heed the results of this experiment we've been through, we are dooming ourselves to an even worse fate in the future. And we'd be passing up a crucial opportunity to drastically *improve* the world – to find a new sense of passion, vitality, vivacity, vigor, and verve, beyond what we even imagined.

In a nutshell, that's why we should care. So what should we do about it? In a nutshell, I hope you read on, sit with the insights and questions that arise, talk about them with others, and plug into the post-pandemic effort.

My goal here is to provide a Roadmap to Recovery we can all use. So let's start with start with some key terms that can guide us going forward:

> ➤ From Pandemic Era to <u>Recovery Era</u> –from there we can launch into the Passionate Era
>
> ➤ From Greater Resignation to <u>Greater Reengagement and Reimagination</u>
>
> ➤ Moving On with Business-as-Usual to <u>Moving Through with Transitional Ceremonies</u>

Each chapter in this book will focus on specific, tangible actions that go into these. Think of this introduction as the high-level, big-picture concepts that can help us organize the rest of our practical steps – the boundaries and compass of the Roadmap to Recovery...

From Pandemic Era to Recovery Era

After going through three years of a Pandemic Era, we now need a few years – maybe more than three, maybe less – of a Recovery Era. By capitalizing this term, I hope to highlight the ideal scale of the Recovery Era, as a concerted social response to the coronavirus – a public health program like any other that's cropped up in response to COVID.

In the Pandemic Era we addressed the immediate impact of the virus with masking, vaccines, social distancing, working and learning from home, etc. In the Recovery Era we'll address the pandemic's *ongoing* impact, with efforts designed around the lessons illustrated in this book.[5] Ideally, we need to think on this large scale, in order to adequately respond to the toll and legacy of the pandemic.

That said, even if we fall short of a massive, coordinated national or global healing project, individuals, families, organizations, and institutions can still adopt their own *Recovery Era mentality*. This will be especially helpful and needed as we support vulnerable people in our lives – bereaved people, frontline workers, children and elders, people with disabilities and people from under-resourced communities. The chapters ahead are essentially a playbook for the Recovery Era mentality. This is how we pave the way to a Passionate Era.

It's important here to make a distinction: *relief* is not the same as *recovery*. Both are part of the healing process, but relief only goes as far as, "good thing we stopped the bleeding!" Recovery takes the necessary next step of, "now we need to clean, sew up, and bandage the wound, so it doesn't keep reopening and getting infected." Relief settles for a mentality of, "well, I guess this looks... fine... enough – I hope it stays that way!" Recovery opts for the mentality of, "let's do this right and make sure it's fixed."

From Greater Resignation to Greater Reengagement & Reimagination

One of the big social upheavals instigated by the pandemic is, of course, the Great Resignation.[6] Millions of workers have left their jobs, whether due to insufficient pay, flexibility, respect, advancement opportunities, or life balance. Many more (like me) found the last few years to be the right time to follow their Soul's calling toward their ideal work – hence why a friend and colleague of mine refers also to the Great *Reimagination*.[7] This has all added up to a headache for employers, but the benefits for workers indicate it's a net-positive and overdue phenomenon.

Riffing off this terminology of the Great Resignation, I've identified another phenomenon that isn't so encouraging. I call it the Great*er* Resignation: declining mental-emotional-spiritual health and community cohesion in the U.S.; increasing depression, anxiety, despair, isolation, loneliness, escapism, animosity, polarization, and inequality.[8,9,10,11]

More and more people are feeling hopeless about the way the world is heading.[12] I think comedian Bo Burnham spoke as well and as tragically as anyone to this gloomy zeitgeist, in his landmark 2021 film and Pandemic Era time-capsule, *Inside*.[13] These trends were all undoubtedly in play long before 2020, but COVID-19 exacerbated them. They threaten to hang like a dark cloud over the future, effectively extending the Pandemic Era for many more years to come. Unless we intervene.

To counteract the Greater Resignation, the Recovery Era requires at its center a Greater *Reengagement*. Collectively and individually, we need to at least *double* our efforts at building belonging and relationships. We must reinvigorate a sense of membership in society and innovate new community projects. And at the same time we must lean into my friend's notion of a Greater *Reimagination*, at least *doubling* our efforts to nurture an attitude of courage and imagine hopeful futures, whether via works of art or simply in our conversations with others. By approaching the Recovery Era in this way, we hasten the arrival of the Passionate Era.

From Moving On with Business-as-Usual to Moving Through with Transitional Ceremonies

How do we start moving from Pandemic Era to Recovery Era, from Greater Resignation to Greater Reengagement and Reimagination? We'll explore the particulars in upcoming chapters. But in general, we have to abandon the fantasy of moving *on*, instead adopting the ethos of *Moving Through*. And we have to interrupt our slide into illusory business-as-usual with what I call *Transition Ceremonies*: special, set-aside contexts to acknowledge, process, and honor the Pandemic Era, and reorient to the Recovery Era.

To understand the difference between moving on and moving through – and between greater resignation and greater reengagement – we can look to examples from history, and from our own lives over these last few years.

The COVID-19 pandemic was unprecedented in so many ways. But, as I mentioned previously, it does fit into a larger category of worldwide communal traumatic experiences. And, for better or worse, we have been through those before. I've been especially struck by the parallels and lessons from recent precedents, which we'll explore here:

1. The 1918-1920 Pandemic and Post-WW1 Crisis: how to fail at recovery

2. The Post-WW2 Crisis: how to succeed at recovery

And even more so than these sweeping historical narratives, our own personal narratives – including our own experiences with trauma – can inform our perspective on what we need to learn from the past. We'll explore one of my own experiences in this introduction as well:

3. Loss in the Time of COVID: the lingering pain of obstructed grief, and how to redeem it

These three examples each offer their own insights on the questions and roadmap outlined above. Each offers a powerful lens through which we can look at our task at hand of Recovery, Reengagement, Reimagination, and Moving Through. As you read through what I'm learning, I invite you to reflect on what you can learn from histories you know yourself, and from your own intimate stories...

The 1918–1920 Pandemic and Post–WW1 Crisis:
How to Fail at Recovery

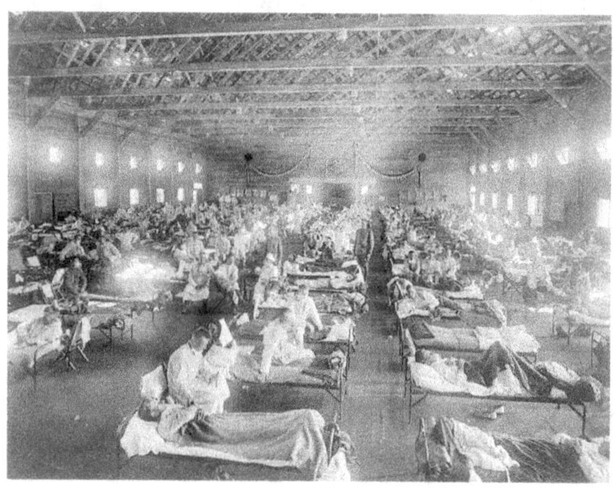

The last COVID-scale pandemic lasted from approximately February 1918 to April 1920, as the world struggled with a strain of the influenza virus, typically misnamed the "Spanish flu."[14] This coincided with the end of the First World War:

> the final Armistice (or ceasefire) between the Allies and Germany was signed on 11 Nov. 1918,

> the Treaty of Versailles (officially ending the war) was signed on 28 Jun. 1919, and

> the Paris Peace Conference (further negotiations) concluded on 21 Jan. 1920.[15,16,17]

It's generally estimated that as many as 50 million from the disease and WWI together, 15-25 million people per catastrophe. To say the least, the duration of the war was horrific, the end was protracted, the overlap with the virus was tragic, and the lack of public health systems to accommodate victims of either calamity was glaring. Considering these daunting facts, we may be prone to let our forebears off the hook for how they responded. How did they respond?

By almost every measure, badly. To focus on the actions in which the U.S. was involved:

> For the eight months from the Armistice until the Treaty of Versailles, the Allies (Americans, British, French, etc.) blockaded German ports, effectively killing hundreds of thousands of people with starvation and disease.[18]

> Then in the Treaty and Conference process, the Allies extracted punitive reparations from Germany, drastically more than the defeated empire was capable of paying (the final payment wasn't made until 2010, 90 years later).[19]

To Germans at the time, and to historians thereafter, these actions were understood as mostly vengeful rather than strategic in any significant way.[20] They are widely regarded as having sown seeds of resentment among the German people, toward the Allies and toward the leaders of the German Weimar Republic who complied with them. The acrimony was stoked even further when this all precipitated the cratering of the German economy in 1921-23, in which many people had to barter so they wouldn't starve.[21]

By 1933, these seeds had grown into the newly installed Nazi regime. Soon the Allies found themselves fighting with Germany once again – in the most destructive war in human history. And none of this is to excuse the Germans – they of course abetted the scourge of fascism. Everyone in every country was desperate, yet everyone made decisions.

Given all this self-sabotage, it's perhaps not surprising that, throughout the three decades from the beginning of World War 1 to the end of World War 2, little was done on any large scale to proactively help *anyone* recover from either the Great War or the pandemic.[22] Some people were able to partake in the short-lived Roaring 20's

– a time of compensatory partying, which did help people cope to some degree.[23] But many more fell into the Lost Generation – millions now stranded in quiet desperation, addiction, grief, and rootlessness, susceptible to the lure of rising totalitarianism.[24]

Rather than confront the deeper, shared emotional and spiritual reality of what everyone had been through, the response to the 1918-1920 Pandemic and Post-WWI Crisis was a mere slide into dissociation, with a side of scapegoating to gloss things over. And without a healthy process to address grief and rekindle passion, these emotions were pushed underground – only to come back with a vengeance. We opted for *relief* rather than recovery, and paid a ruinous price.

In summary, to use our terminology from above:

> ➢ The Pandemic-and-WW1 Era effectively lingered on for decades despite being "over."

> ➢ There was a Greater Resignation: declining mental-emotional-spiritual health and community cohesion; increasing depression, anxiety, despair, isolation, loneliness, escapism, animosity, polarization, and inequality.

> ➢ "Moving on" and "business-as-usual" proved to be illusions, soon giving way to a backlash worse than what anyone could have imagined.

Unfortunately, it took the crisis of World War 2 to teach us the error of our ways. Fortunately, we did learn.

The Post-WW2 Crisis: How to Succeed at Recovery

The aftermath of the Second World War is one of those rare, inspiring stories in human history, proving that our species – even the most powerful people among us – *can* learn from our mistakes and build a better world.

To say the least, there was much to rebuild. A staggering 70-85 million people lost their lives in the Second World War. Much of Europe and East Asia lay in ruins, struggling with food shortages and poverty. Considering these daunting facts, it might've been understandable if our forebears had mounted an inadequate response. So how did they respond?

In almost every way, much better than after WWI. The most notable response was, of course, the Marshall Plan:

> ➢ From 1948 to 1952, the U.S. disbursed $11.8 billion in grants and $1.5 billion in loans (that's in 1948 dollars – $115 billion total in 2021 dollars) to European countries to rebuild their housing and infrastructure, and get people working and eating again.

> ➢ During that same time it also disbursed about half as much to East Asian countries, though these weren't officially considered part of the Marshall Plan.[25]

This stimulated unprecedented economic, political, and demographic recovery and growth, quickly enabling all recipient nations advance well beyond their pre-war vitality. It also helped lay the groundwork for what would become the North Atlantic Treaty Organization (NATO) and the European Union (EU) – permanently preventing another apocalyptic war in Western Europe.

Prevention of such a war was the ultimate purpose of the plan. Everyone saw clearly how the harsh, retributive actions of the Allies after World War One and demonization of Germany had incubated fascism, paving the way for the horrors of World War Two. This time around, the U.S. and other nations set out to prove that forgiveness, generosity, and reintegration were the only way to healing, peace, and progress. And prove it we did.

On a smaller scale, the recovery effort of the city of London is just as stirring. The 1940-41 Blitz (or Bombing of London) destroyed or damaged vast swaths of almost every neighborhood, killed over 30,000 people, and threatened to hobble Britain's morale.[26]
Winston Churchill is often credited with rousing the nation's gumption with his speeches during this time, but even more so, he was responding to a collective mood that was already present among the citizenry. Amidst the devastation, ordinary people were organizing in a grassroots effort, block-by-block, neighborhood-by-neighborhood, to rescue the wounded, bury the dead, clean up and rebuild the city, and support each other.[27]

Despite so many people being traumatized, psychological research demonstrated that, compared to before the bombing, the communal recovery campaign *improved* people's mental health overall and *reduced* anti-social behaviors across the board (addiction, crime, suicide, etc.). These positive effects lasted long after the war, and galvanized a visionary spirit of British resilience. We've seen a similar pattern with community responses to other disasters, including the 9/11 terrorist attacks and Hurricane Katrina.[28]

Rather than give into inertia and condemnation as we did with the previous crisis, the response to the Post-WW2 Crisis envisioned a larger definition of shared humanity and repair. We coordinated a conscious outpouring of aid, to prevent another crisis and ensure an optimistic future. We faced our grief, tapped into passion, and channeled them constructively. We embraced *recovery* over relief, helped heal our history, and laid an enduring foundation.

In summary, to use our terminology introduced above:

> - The Marshall Plan helped end the WW2 Era and activate a *Recovery Era*.
> - The healing of London indicated a *Greater Reengagement and Reimagination* happening for people around the world.
> - Both efforts proved that *moving through* a worldwide communal trauma is the only real way forward.

In response to the coronavirus pandemic, I believe we ideally need a recovery effort on the scale of the Marshall Plan – a global restoration of individual and collective wellbeing, and a massive down-payment on growth.

I know that's a tall order. The good news is, even if we can't muster something quite that bold and sweeping, we can still follow the example of Londoners during and after the Blitz. While I think it's a good practice to hold the largest possible vision for recovery, and a top-down strategy may be vital, a bottom-up one is even more so. We

can come together, block-by-block, neighborhood-by-neighborhood, to rebuild health and community. And we must.

But even this grassroots approach requires enormous work. How do we rally enough people to the cause? And how do we ensure people get what they need for their own healing along the way?

I believe Transition Ceremonies hold the key. We need special, set-aside contexts to acknowledge, process, and honor the Pandemic Era, and reorient to the Recovery Era. For many of us, including me, the last few years have hit home just how important these are.

Loss in the Time of COVID: The Lingering Pain of Obstructed Grief, and How to Redeem It

When the pandemic first hit the U.S. in Spring 2020, I resolved to face it with an attitude of resilience, courage, and hope. I focused intently on reaching out to friends, family, coworkers, and strangers, trying to infuse humor and encouragement into every interaction, meeting stories of loneliness and hardship with an open heart. It felt good to take on that role, and it came naturally to me. Until I found out a friend of mine was dying.

In June 2020, COVID killed my friend, Marny. She'd been in the hospital, fighting the virus for months as she recovered from surgery. She was 31. Now I found myself fighting to stay resilient, courageous, hopeful, to muster any humor, encouragement, or an open heart. Suddenly, every day was a genuine struggle.

Like so many of us during the pandemic, her loved ones had to watch from a distance as their beloved Marny declined. Then, like so many families, all her family could manage right after she passed on was a small, intimate memorial. A year later they were able to hold a somewhat bigger gathering, but I and many others still weren't able to be there. So on top of the devastation of her death, we all had to endure a short-circuited grieving process. For my own part, I grieved alone instead, crying in my car many times.

Millions – maybe billions – of people now have stories just like this, and many more have now heard these stories. We've felt the heartbreak of loss, then felt it compounded by the heartbreak of irresolution.

Without ceremony, our grief has been stymied and scattered, splintered and surreal. Without a capstone experience like a memorial or funeral, an essential mile-marker is missing on our life pathway, leaving us with a chronic, low-grade feeling of lost-ness and incompleteness. This is true of other ceremonies we missed too, like graduations, births, weddings, and important birthdays and holidays. We need these sacred contexts to help us acknowledge significant changes, to give important events the honor they deserve. To live well, we need ceremony.

Over time, the experience of obstructed grief for Marny has kindled a new resolution and passion in me. Given the magnitude of pain from the Pandemic Era and the gravity of the transition to the Recovery Era, to live well in the years to come, we need to give the past few years the ceremony they deserve.

The pandemic itself needs a kind of funeral and mourning period. And we need a graduation of sorts too, an ushering in of recovery. This is our gateway to finding our passion once again.

As far as a template for such a ceremony, you can simply work through this book alongside others – as a Recovery Era book club or Post-Pandemic Experience (PPE), if you will! Whatever you decide to do, I hope you put what sticks with you from these Lessons from the Pandemic to good use, and share it with folks you know.

At the time of this writing, I'm also developing what might be the first-ever comprehensive, practical, easily-accessible online courses for helping people process grief – *Guide for the Grief Journey: Ten Touchstones* – and pursue their passion – *Soul Sagas: Finding Our True Callings in Our Life Stories*. Subscribe to the InVocation blog to stay tuned for updates on these, and visit: invitedinvocation.com/grief-journey-guide and invitedinvocation.com/soul-sagas-find-true-life-calling.

We've missed so many memorials these last few years – we can't afford to miss this one. Not just because the un-metabolized, sublimated trauma will continue to plague us, and someday ambush us. But because we need to seize the amazing opportunity presented by the Pandemic Era: this is the first time in the hundred years since the last pandemic that everyone on planet Earth has endured a relatively similar hardship.

We've never had such fertile ground for a global conversation about how to grieve well, a global conversation about how inspire passion, a global healing and unifying process. After being thrashed by the upheaval of the pandemic, we could now right ourselves, and write a new chapter of history.

Ceremonies won't fix all our post-pandemic problems, but they are vital to a resilient, courageous, hopeful future. I still feel the pain of losing Marny, and the rest of the many millions killed by COVID. I still feel my obstructed grief for her, for them, and for all of us still mourning. But I've found that advocating for Transition Ceremonies and this Roadmap to Recovery is helping me honor Marny's memory, carry her unshakable, joyful fighting-spirit forward, and redeem that pain and grief. I hope that by joining me in this work, you too can find redemption. And I hope we can invite the rest of the world into the same.

In summary, to use our terminology introduced above:

> ➤ *Transition Ceremonies* can be the pivot point – from Pandemic Era to Recovery Era, from Greater Resignation to Greater Reengagement and Reimagination – helping us move through our pain and grief into redemption and passion.

Now that we can better hold our history and stories in perspective, we turn back to the question: What do we do about all of this? What tangible, concrete steps can we all take? What are the ingredients that go into a Recovery Era, Greater Reengagement and Reimagination, moving through, and Transitional Ceremonies?

The Ten Touchstones of Grief

Drawing on many observations, conversations, research, and InVocation's community pandemic recovery work, I've identified ten basic practices we can all engage, to help move through emotions that come with the grief process The pandemic taught me and others I've met about what I call the Ten Touchstones of Grief.[29]

What is a "touchstone?" Back before human beings had compasses and maps, we navigated the land with rocks as road markers. If you were blazing a new trail, you'd arrange these stones as guidelines and landmarks. That way, people coming after could find safe passage through the wilderness, without having to continually reinvent the path and face the same dangers all over again.

That's a pretty apt metaphor for where we are right now as a species. And as we face the post-pandemic wilderness, in one sense, we have been here before, as we saw in our examples from history and our stories. We now need to follow the touchstones of our ancestors. In another sense, we are very much in unprecedented territory. To help ourselves and future generations find the route through the next crisis, we need to memorize in real-time the right way through, laying touchstones everyone will be thankful for later.

Each Touchstone I lay out is comprised of two components: a difficulty that comes up in the grief process (whether your process related to the pandemic or not), and a simple spiritual practice that helps us move through it. And these practices help us get through more than just grief – they generally help us just get through *life*, whether we're in good times or hard times. They are all easy, concrete things we can do to keep finding wellbeing, balance, and meaning, to remind ourselves what really matters on a day-to-day basis.

These are grouped into two larger categories, based on two basic human needs. We'll unpack all of the above in the chapters ahead:

The Need for Catharsis: spiritual & emotional resolution				
Moving through	numbness & silence	with	1.	storytelling
	doubt & despair		2.	time in Nature
	anger & conflictedness		3.	creative projects (like arts & crafts)
	sorrow & sadness		4.	eulogizing
Moving into	gratitude, hope, & purpose	with	5.	intention-setting

The Need for Support Structures: restoring a sense of time & place, relationships, & community				
Moving through	disorientation into reorientation	by	6.	finding sacred times
			7.	finding sacred places
	disconnection (depression, anxiety, fear, isolation, loneliness, escapism, & bitterness) into reconnection	by	8.	returning to radical presence
			9.	returning to "village-life"
			10.	centering the margins

PART 1: CATHARSIS

<u>The Need for Catharsis</u>

Every single one of us has been through a lot these past few years.

The virus struck suddenly. Our daily rhythms disappeared or shifted dramatically. We lived in limbo, waiting for vaccines and clear guidance, the next barrage of bad news and the glimmer of good, waiting for the chance to see and touch those we loved. Then, ever since the world first closed down, reopening has been slow and messy, a sense of normalcy elusive.

Throughout this Pandemic Era, humanity has – we and our loved ones have – suffered greatly. Millions have died. The rest of us have had to watch, struggling to figure out how to cope, how to mourn. Our bereaved, our frontline workers, our kids and elders – all of us – have been deprived of essential experiences, asked to make sacrifices we weren't ready to make. We've all had to stifle painful emotions. We've all become familiar with fight-flight-or-freeze modes of existence, cycling in and out of them, feeling them in varying intensities. In other words, we've endured trauma.

And the chaos of it all has left us at a loss for understanding. We've been contending with forces of Nature and society and mortality, forces we don't fully comprehend. How do we make sense of it all? If we want to believe love and justice and a Higher Power give order to our world, how then do we explain the tragedy of the pandemic? Is a hopeful narrative possible? Thus, in addition to trauma, we've endured a crisis of meaning.

In the aftermath of hardships like this, we human beings need *catharsis.*[1]

This term comes from the Greek word for "cleansing." As with a bodily cleansing, the first step of an emotional and spiritual cleansing is to release what has become stuck and stagnated. When you scrape your knee, you have to clean out the gravel before it can heal. Likewise, we now need to express what we have repressed or denied or left un-felt, say the things and ask the questions we've held onto all this time.

Only then can we experience the second step of catharsis: a sense of resolution and closure, and from there, a sense of forward momentum and the renewal of passion we seek.

So what have we repressed or denied or left un-felt? And what is the best way to release it?
How do we take the first step?

<u>Touchstone 1</u>: Moving through Numbness and Silence with <u>Storytelling</u>

First we must clear the obstacle that's blocking everything else we need to express: our silence and numbness regarding what we've been through.

We all want to move on from the Pandemic Era, put the pain behind us. But as we covered in the introduction, it's not that simple, nor even possible – we can only move *through*. The cost of forgetting is too high. We must remember, together. It begins with melting the numbness and silence that has us frozen. If we can start talking about the Pandemic Era, soon our emotions about it will thaw, and the Recovery Era can flow from there.

Just talking about the pandemic… where do we begin?

> We need to tell each other our stories of the Pandemic Era.

In my life and work, I can testify that simply speaking about our unspoken experiences to others is a powerful act of healing. It frees what was once imprisoned in us, and invites others to free themselves too. And it doesn't need to be an exhaustive or overwhelming chronicle of the past few years – a little storytelling goes a long way.

> And we need to tell a *variety* of stories.

To repeat a previous understatement – we've been through a lot these past few years. Pain and goodness, confusion and clarity. As we start to recover and make sense of this era, we want to foster openness, embracing the fullest extent of what we have to learn. If we fixate too much on either negative or positive narratives, we risk losing a larger perspective on what has been a multi-dimensional experience. We risk crowding out

wisdom we hadn't considered from other people's stories. It's vital to create hospitality in our storytelling. When we do, we create hospitality for the gamut of emotions we need to express.

You can use the blank pages in the back of the book, for this and the other Touchstones. Here are some storytelling prompts you can use to reflect on and share your own stories:

Getting Our Bearings

- What was the beginning of the pandemic like for you?

- What were some of the people and experiences that got you through the pandemic? What was so helpful about these?

- What did you do for your sanity or self-care?

- Who were some of the people you cared for in the last few years? Can you think of any special moments you shared with them? What encouragement would these people have for you?

- What are some media (music, books, movies, TV, art, games, crafts, etc.) you connected with? Explore why.

Hardship and Beauty

- Reflecting back on the last few years – since the beginning of 2020, what have been 3 of the most difficult experiences you've personally been through? What emotions did these bring up for you at the time? What do you feel now as you reflect on them?

- Reflecting back on the last few years – since the beginning of 2020, what have been 3 of the best experiences you've personally had? What emotions did these bring up for you at the time? What do you feel now as you reflect on them?

- When was a time you got to let your emotions out? When have you felt moments of release?

- When are some times in the last few years you've experienced hope, kindness, or a sense of sacredness?

- What are some funny or surprising stories you've held onto?

Touchstone 2: Moving through Doubt and Despair with Time in Nature

Once we're created some room for difficult emotions to come up, one that might surface is doubt, particularly doubt that the future is hopeful and that the Divine is helping us get there. And when doubt lingers in our consciousness for long enough without enough reasons for hope, it turns into despair.

These are hallmarks of a crisis of meaning. With the devastation caused by the coronavirus and our social reaction to it, how can we trust that the world is headed in a good direction? And how can we trust that Someone is steering the ship?

I believe that, despite the reality of suffering, there is always a compelling rationale for faith in the future and the Divine.[2] But I also believe mere rationality – whether based on religion, secular philosophy, or even clear-eyed spirituality – usually provides cold comfort. For our faith to take root and reassure us, we need *experiences* that nurture it.[3] In our age of such dissolution and disillusionment, where do we turn for such experiences?

> ➢ I always advocate relationships, community, and art as reliable places to find encouragement. But even more so, I recommend time in Nature.

Our planet, down to each person's local environment, is vibrantly alive with the incarnate presence of the Divine. Every sound is a note in the symphony of Creation. Every smell is a flavor in the Earth's great banquet. Every naturally textured-and-colored surface is a mirror of Spirit, our individual Souls, and the Sacredness of the biosphere. The wild world is undeniably and irrepressibly beautiful. And a living testament to a loving Creator.

> ➢ Especially in our times of doubt and despair, when no work or word of human origin can give us solace, the best thing we can do is go wandering-and-wondering in Nature.[4]
>
> ➢ You can find more tips on how to do this wa/ondering well on the InVocation website: invitedinvocation.com/blog/categories/holyear-holydays.
>
> ➢ In addition, I recommend that, when in search of something true to believe in, you seek out (either or both) Nature's *intimacy* and *grandeur*.

Look for beauty in the small and understated – there you will find the intricate, self-regenerating artistry of the living world. Look for beauty in the big and breathtaking – there you will find the epic, humbling sweep of time and the elements. In both cases, it will be hard not to feel delight and awe at your own bigness and smallness in the cosmic tapestry. And maybe even at the One who wove it, made it all – including you – with such fierce, tender love and care.

> ➢ Remain there as long as you can. If you watch, listen, feel for long enough, you may just notice Someone watching, listening, feeling you right back.
>
> ➢ Bring your questions. From how to find meaning in the pandemic, to how to find meaning in life – the Guide will have guidance for you when you are ready to receive it.
>
> ➢ And share your story about the experience. Even if it's something you keep between yourself and the living world, I hope you find ways to let the story live through you. This is how we create a future worth believing in.

Here's one of my own stories of a Pandemic Era wa/ondering.

In June 2020, in the wake of my friend Marny passing on from COVID, the murder of George Floyd, and the protests in my hometown of Minneapolis, I spent a day and night in solitude at Sun Lakes Dry Falls State Park in central Washington. The park rests in an ancient canyon – a desert oasis surrounded by rocky, lichen-encrusted cliffs. I wa/ondered around for hours, at first taking in the magnificent beauty, then eventually crying and praying: "Where are you? Are you with us?"

I found myself walking under a cliff. All along the canyon walls, there were piles of jagged stones, eroded and fallen from their perches above. One fell near me as I cried out. I looked up.

I saw a face. The natural features of the rock looked like a huge, carved face, gazing down at me. It looked deeply sad, like it had been crying too.

I realized it was. The fallen stone had been a tear, the pile of stones on which I stood, a great hill of tears. All along the canyon, miles of mountains of tears. And above them, thousands of faces. All weeping.

Weeping for the suffering of humankind. Crying for the destruction wrought by the virus. Crying for the destruction wrought by racism. Crying for George and for Marny and their loved ones. Crying for us. Crying with us. I could now almost hear the silent sobs of the Earth, of the Spirit, echoing around the canyon, vowing to help us heal. I added my tears to the canyon's, and made the same vow.

Where will your wa/ondering take you?

Touchstone 3: Moving through Anger and Conflictedness with Creative Projects

Another source of inner turmoil is our anger and conflictedness about the pandemic and its collateral damage.

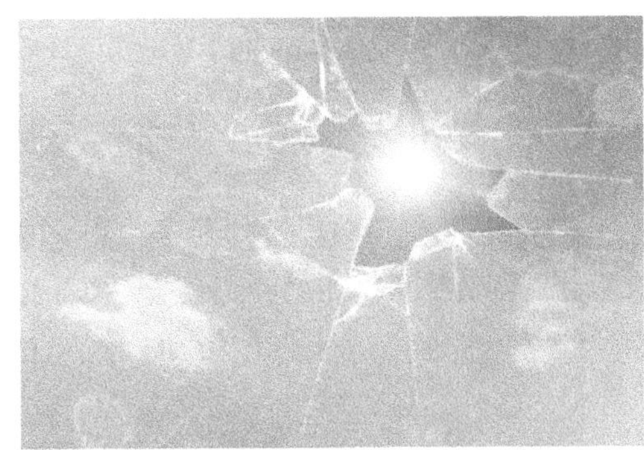

Considering everything we've been through, we can all easily find reasons to feel upset. Whatever our political persuasions, we can all point to individual and institutional failures and frustrations from this time. Maybe we even harbor a more existential resentment, toward the virus itself, or toward Nature or our Higher Power for allowing this crisis to happen.

And as is often the case with anger, it may be messy and complicated. We may feel guilty about our emotions, questioning whether they're fair, and how, in spite of everything, to forgive. Thus we can be torn, conflicted.

Whatever the case, nowadays there are few, if any, places we can express these fraught feelings to their fullest extent. In part that's because our culture so readily conflates anger with blame, and hesitancy with weakness. We're encouraged to locate ultimate responsibility for our pain in some (usually convenient) target, then to punish or ostracize them, without mercy or a second thought. The truth we know deep down is that this rarely brings us satisfaction, let alone justice. And if our anger or the target of our ire is deemed *in*convenient or taboo, we're expected to stifle our emotions altogether.

We ultimately want repair rather than retribution or repression. We want our and others' anger to be a constructive force, not a destructive one. And we want the complexity of our emotional lives to be honored.

So how do we manage anger constructively, and honor conflictedness?

> ➢ We need to give these emotions a creative outlet.

In my experience, most people lose their cool when merely speaking or hearing about these unsavory feelings, quickly collapsing a conversation. On the other hand, when we get to experience our and others' anger and conflictedness via a creative medium (like arts and crafts), there's much more room to breathe.

A poem, letter, song, drawing, or other artifact, infused with our emotions, becomes a vessel for them, holding them on our behalf. The anger and conflictedness get displaced from us directly. This enables us and others to observe and interact with them more objectively and graciously than we otherwise would. With these emotions that can get so up in our faces, this puts them at arms-length, helping everyone feel safer and more productive in the conversation about them.

I've seen that channeling our anger and conflictedness creatively also allows us to be more raw, yet more refined at the same time. These emotions can be as hard to express as they are to hear about, and we can get tripped up by overwhelm and taboos when we speak to them. Listeners can also become reactive around them, prone to interruption while we sort through the already-thorny problem of how to articulate ourselves well.

But when we consolidate our whole messy message in one symbolic representation, we're able to communicate in one fell swoop. The poem, letter, song, drawing, etc. – there it is, how you feel, all in one place. Then people who witness what you've made can absorb your point more contemplatively, and if they have questions, they can ask them more open-heartedly.

Here are some creative prompts you can use to make and share your own project:

<u>Pick your message</u>

- ➢ Are you still carrying anger or conflictedness from the Pandemic Era? What about?

- ➢ How would you ideally want to express these feelings?

<u>Pick your medium</u>

- ➢ Think about some of your favorite hobbies, arts and crafts – is there a way to express your fraught emotions through these? What comes to mind when you imagine a creative project that communicates how you feel.

<u>Create your project</u>

- ➢ Use art, craft, and any other supplies to make creative expressions of the anger or conflictedness you're carrying in the wake of the pandemic. Again, the purpose here is to honor these feelings, while helping them find dynamic creativity rather than becoming stagnant.

- ➢ You might, for instance:
    - ○ Write a letter, a poem, or the dialogue of a conflict you've had or want to have.
    - ○ Write the name of someone in power or someone who's died on an old t-shirt; use cardboard and marker to make a sword and shield, or some chaotic squiggles.
    - ○ Create something more involved, e.g. a drawing, painting, song, dance, sculpture, etc.

<u>Share your project</u>

- ➢ Along the way, I encourage you to discuss these projects with others. Head to the InVocation website for a video on how to run a *sharing circle*, where people can express themselves with minimum judgment and maximum respect and authenticity: invitedinvocation.com/post/sharing-circle. You can use this for storytelling and other Touchstones too!

Touchstone 4: Moving through Sorrow and Sadness with Eulogizing

Sorrow and sadness may be the most obvious emotions we're carrying from the Pandemic Era, and we hardly need to recount more reasons why than we already have in this book. What might not be so obvious, however, is what we *do* with our grief.

How can we create adequate catharsis for our most painful emotion?

From my life and work, I've realized what I now consider a sacred principle: grief and the grieving process are unique, individualized experiences for everyone.[5] Each person must listen deeply to what their particular sorrow and sadness asks of them, and as much as possible, act only on that. There is no formula or template, and any attempt to impose one does injustice to the Soul.

Yet I've also seen that, as we move through sorrow and sadness, our culture harms the Soul just as much in its failure to provide sufficient options and guidance. We can walk the path of hardship without external leading, and can even do stretches of it alone – but that doesn't mean we can or should go without any help whatsoever. It's self-defeating to attempt to bootstrap grief.

So I hold this as a sacred principle too: grief and the grieving process are only possible with support. While there is no paved road, it's essential for us to have a sense of the resources and healing practices available to us on our way.

What are these healing practices on the grief journey? I believe our best answer is to look at the wisdom accrued across as many cultures as possible, across the longest span of time. What practices have humans everywhere, throughout our history, found helpful? Our common heritage indicates at the very least:

➢ Time and space for the grievers to be in solitude, with intimate loved ones, and among broader community – we cover this in Touchstones 6-10

➢ Rituals in each of these three contexts to honor the sacredness of the person (or experience) that has passed, e.g. a funeral/memorial and mourning period – we covered this in the Introduction, discussing Transition Ceremonies

➢ Opportunities for grievers in each of these contexts to speak to the legacy of the person (or experience) that has passed – a eulogy

Contrary to popular belief, eulogies shouldn't necessarily be purely positive narratives – they are often more powerful when they can articulate pain and complexity as well (as any eulogy from the last few years may need to).

Nor do they have to be in the form of a speech – they can be expressed as a letter or a story, written but unspoken, or rely on languages other than words, like music or visual or tactile art. They don't even need to be original, relying instead on the language of others, like a playlist, poem, performance, or movie testifying to one's feelings.

The only requirements are that they are truthful, given from the heart of the one in sorrow, and received by hearers with a spirit of generosity. Such honesty is healing; the truth sets us free.

> ➢ As we move into the Recovery Era, we can all benefit by crafting eulogies of the Pandemic Era.

This can help us honor people and experiences we've personally lost these last few years, as well as ones we've seen others lose. It can help us find our way through the wilderness of sorrow, and eventually come out the other side.

> ➢ And so much the better if we can deliver these in the company of loved ones or community, and in the context of an acknowledged funeral, memorial, or mourning period.

We can multiply the potential for transformation by creating a special occasion for us to witness and be witnessed in each other's grief. My recommendation is to simply host people around a bonfire, and give anyone who has a eulogy the chance to read it.

Here are some prompts you can use to create and share a eulogy:

> ### Writing
>
> ➢ Are you still carrying sorrow or sadness from the Pandemic Era? What about? Was there someone or something you lost? Is there a burden still weighing you down?
>
> ➢ What comes to mind when you imagine writing in depth about how you feel? If you lost someone, what comes to mind when you imagine writing a tribute to them?
>
> ➢ Have you been able to express your feelings about this? How would you ideally want to express these feelings? What would be honoring to that person or experience, and to yourself?

<u>Sharing</u>

➢ After your bonfire or other gathering, your group can talk about grief as an ongoing journey, holding sacred the memory of this experience, holding prayers and love for everyone our sorrow touches. It's a good practice to leave spaces for silence in this process.

➢ Beyond this, in an upcoming online course on working through grief – *Guide for the Grief Journey: Ten Touchstones* – we'll walk through the steps of crafting a eulogy in depth.[6] Subscribe to the InVocation blog to stay tuned for updates on that course.

None of this, however, guarantees a straightforward process. Grief cannot somehow be resolved in one momentous event. We may need to courageously return to the pain, to the eulogy, to rituals, maybe many times. We must continue to listen to our sorrow and sadness and follow where they lead. If we do, we can be sure it leads toward a new and better horizon...

Touchstone 5: Moving into Gratitude, Hope, and Purpose with Intention-Setting

So far we've discussed catharsis mainly as release and resolution for troublesome, heavy emotions. But we must also have a chance to release our buoyant emotions too, our gratitude, hope, and purpose.

Despite all the trials and tribulations of the Pandemic Era, we've all gotten to experience these uplifting feelings as well, even if only for moments at a time. Maybe you have a new appreciation for your health, home, Nature, relationships, work, or the essential workers that make our lives possible. Maybe you've been inspired by people's heroism, or by the support of community. Maybe you want to find a way to make new friends, focus on your creativity, or help people recover from the pandemic.

These emotions too must be honored and expressed. Just as much as with doubt, anger, and sorrow, if our gladness and optimism remain trapped, it can diminish us. If we liberate them, they bring renewal and forward momentum, reinvigorating us with the passion we need. Indeed, gratitude, hope, and purpose are what all our turmoil *resolves into*, and even if we don't yet feel complete resolution, we can still nurture goodness in our lives.

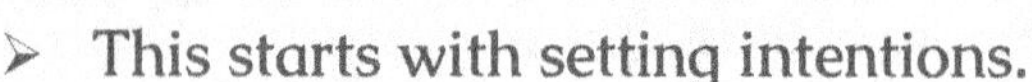

So how do we nourish our gratitude, hope, and purpose?

Sometimes these feelings arise in us spontaneously, in which case, we can just lean into and appreciate them. However, these spikes of positivity tend to wear off quickly. The more troublesome emotions can hijack our attention, or we can simply get sidetracked with the busyness and routines of life. To make sure we leave room for an ongoing connection to gratitude, hope, and purpose, we do ourselves a huge favor by actively, consciously focusing on them.

> ➢ This starts with setting intentions.

We take proactive time to identify what we're grateful for, our hopes, and our goals. We make lists. We treat them as resolutions, commit to holding to them. Thus we plant a memorable flag in the ever-flowing tide of life, something we can always swim back to.

> ➢ Then we maintain our intentions.

We keep our lists in places that are easily accessible amidst the hurly-burly of our life, places we often visit in our daily rhythm. We continue checking back in with ourselves on them. We keep swimming back to the flag.

> ➢ All the while, we stay in accountability with others.

We keep checking back in with trusted people on what we're each grateful for, our hopes, and our goals. We support one another's commitment to the intentions. We keep each other from losing sight of the flag.

Like with swimming, the more we practice this, the easier it gets, and the easier it is to rebound when we face adversity or inertia again. Furthermore, by setting and holding to our intentions, especially when we do so in community, we kindle new visions for the Recovery Era and the Greater Reengagement.

By setting intentions for ourselves, we may find we're also setting intentions for something much bigger. We're participating in the Greater Reimagination, and therefore setting the stage for the world we'll be creating on the other side of recovery.

Here are some prompts you can use to reflect on and share your own intentions:

<u>Embracing Our Wholeness</u>

> What growth have you experienced these past few years in terms of your health practices – physical, emotional/mental, and spiritual?

> Going forward, what specific goals or intentions do you have around these categories of health practices?

> Going forward, what are your hopes for how others, and our broader world (communities, culture, institutions, etc.), engages these?

<u>Embracing Our Belonging</u>

> What growth have you experienced these past few years in your value of relationships and community?

> Going forward, what specific goals or intentions do you have around your relationships and community?

> Going forward, what are your hopes for how others, and our broader world (communities, culture, institutions, etc.), engages these?

<u>Embracing Our Passion</u>

> What growth have you experienced these past few years in terms of your work, playfulness, and creativity?

> Going forward, what specific goals or intentions do you have around your work, playfulness, and creativity?

> Going forward, what are your hopes for how others, and our broader world (communities, culture, institutions, etc.), engages these?

PART 2: SUPPORT STRUCTURES

The Need for Support Structures

As we covered in the previous chapters, catharsis is essential to Recovery, Reengagement, and Reimagination. But it's not enough. If we pursue only momentary cathartic release and resolution, without practices that can sustain it over the long-haul, we're likely to keep finding ourselves back in the painful place where we started.

We have to address the underlying, lingering reasons why we need to move through numbness, despair, anger, and sorrow in the first place. And collectively, we need a clear, shared set of habits on which we're mutually focusing our intention-setting and our passion. *(We may also need new social programs and initiatives to manage the effects of this virus and prevent the next one. These too are support structures, but I'll leave other writers to argue for them. In this book we're staying focused on simple actions everyone can engage in, starting today.)*

In other words, we must revive the supportive elements that give structure to our lives for catharsis to have staying power. And to find out what these are, we need only look at some of what we lost out on in the Pandemic Era.

Reorientation: Restoring a Sense of Time and Place

Everyone on Earth underwent major disruptions in their everyday rhythm and environments during the pandemic. When the virus first hit, we were suddenly exiled from our spacious, consistent contexts for community, education, and work, and now confined to our homes, vehicles, and screens. While this new, streamlined way of life provided some conveniences in the short-run, we all felt the effects as time dragged on.

We became cramped and cut-off in our isolated little bubbles. "COVID-time" or "COVID-brain" became common, referring to our inability to string events together in a coherent way. For many of us, it was like we were experiencing the world through a prism, and after a while things felt hazy, directionless, and somewhat unreal. The sheer fact that we can designate these years as a distinct "Pandemic Era" – a relative discontinuity in history – speaks to our feeling of disorientation.

Even if it feels like things have stabilized again, it's vital that we consider: Do we truly feel reoriented yet? My guess is we're prone to keep cycling back into dizziness and dazed-ness, unless we *proactively establish* a renewed sense of grounding and regularity.

How do we do this?

Touchstone 6: Finding Sacred Times

Our Lives as Music

We humans relate to time the way we relate to music. Please allow me a poetic parallel here...

For one, we thrive on a sense of rhythm in our days, weeks, months, seasons, and years, the same way we thrive on rhythm in a piece of music. Have you ever tried to listen to a song with a randomized tempo? It is the *definition* of irritating. On the other hand, when we do have a rough idea of what a piece of music – and our time – will hold as it progresses, it helps us focus. This frees our attention for creative expression; we can only really play music, and live deliberately, when there's a steady supporting beat.

We don't, however, like stultifying repetition – a homogenous pattern droning on forever is also a form of torture. Thus we thrive on novelty *paired with consistency*, seeking ways to diversify the *melody* of our lives even while the beat goes on. And while we may love to play several different instruments, each developing the melody in its own distinct way, we can really only play one at a time. So too with our lives: we can best appreciate our various experiences when they aren't all trying to happen at once. We love wild differentiation throughout the course a song or a lifetime, but trying to pack too many notes into one phrase or too many activities into one moment makes for unsatisfying chaos and noise.

Finally, when we have a part of our life's song that's uniquely, extraordinarily beautiful, we want to feature it, give it the soloist's spotlight rather than let it get drowned out by everything else. Celebrations, ceremonies, important anniversaries, birthdays, and holidays – these transcendent moments are what remind us that life is a sacred journey. In music and in everything, we want these *crescendos*.

So if this is what makes for good music and worthwhile time, how would we describe the impact the pandemic has had on these things?

The Pandemic as Noise

In the Pandemic Era, we lost our rhythm, our ability to predict well what's going to happen. What would this schoolyear, the holidays, this quarter, or tomorrow even look like? We lost orientation to these regular patterns of time that structure our lives, orienting instead around the unpredictable number of COVID cases and ever-uncertain headlines. It took a long time for the tempo of our days and weeks to become relatively predictable again, and we're still not quite there with our months, seasons, or years.

Additionally, we lost the melody along with the beat. With the jarring new realities of working and learning from home, social encounters and entertainment restricted to screens, and an eye always on the news, it became harder to recognize distinct activities and truly absorb our experiences. With everything bleeding into everything else and with such split attention, it became harder for us to focus or tap into creativity. And therefore, despite never knowing what was going to happen, we also missed out on the novelty that comes with concentrated exploration of new pursuits. Instead there was a kind of false novelty – too much and yet too little was happening all at once.

On top of it all, we missed out on the special occasions that animate our lives: the graduations, births, weddings, funerals and memorials, important birthdays and holidays. These are the mile-markers that keep us from getting lost on the journey of our lives, the crescendos that shape the song into something memorable. Without these especially sacred moments, our lives have lost a sense of definition.

Together, all these things made the passage of time feel more like noise than like music.

So how do we restore rhythm and focus, novelty and creativity, shape and depth to our lives? How do we find the beat, the melody, the core of our song, and start playing beautifully again?

What We Can Do: Changing Our Tune

I believe we start by reclaiming the transcendent, musical moments. We need a spiritual shock to the system, a reset that reminds us that our time is truly sacred. In other words, we need to be reacquainted with ceremony.

> ➢ This means hosting Transitional Ceremonies – designated times for individuals and communities to process the Pandemic Era and move into the Recovery Era. As far as a template for such a ceremony, you can simply go through this book with a group of people you know – call it a Recovery Era book club or Post-Pandemic Experience (PPE)!
>
> ➢ It also means approaching special occasions in our lives – like graduations, births, weddings, funerals and memorials, important birthdays and holidays – with more intentionality than we ever have before.
>
> ➢ It probably also means establishing national and international COVID-19 Memorials and Memorial Days.

Commemorative events like these will be our most potent tools for reorientation, kickstarting the musicality of our lives once again.

Once we ceremonially restart the music, we can then regain the melody and the beat, which again, we must also remember as sacred.

> ➤ We'll be best served by first experimenting with a variety of spiritual practices that interest us. These could be anything, from the small and simple – a minute of undistracted silence, a word of prayerful gratitude – to the large and involved – like a retreat, class, or program.

> ➤ Then we see if we can establish the optimal rhythm for the ones that suit us best. We ask: what do I need on a daily, weekly, monthly, seasonally, and annual basis to feel grounded?

This is how we unlock our focus and creativity, and keep it unlocked. You can find more of my recommendations on how to find consistency and novelty in spiritual practices on the InVocation website: invitedinvocation.com/post/structure-spirituality-exercises-finding-consistency.[1]

If this all sounds a bit daunting, remember that in any of these cases, you don't have to do it alone!

> ➤ You can join ceremonies and spiritual practices convened by other people, and by existing organizations and institutions. There are all kinds of faith and learning communities out there, hosting all kinds of experiences. These can help you get started, and may even offer you a long-term spiritual home.

> ➤ And at the very least, you can invite a friend into what you're doing, or tag along to what they're doing.

We'll all need to help each other rediscover a sacred orientation to time. Together, we can ensure our lives are soon full of rhythm and focus, novelty and creativity, shape and memorability – beautiful music – again.

Touchstone 7: Finding Sacred Places

Homes, Havens, & Pilgrimages

Just as we humans need consistency, variety, and ceremony in how we experience time, we also need these in how we experience a sense of *place*.

When it comes to our need for consistency, we have a name for the place that serves it best: *home*. We each need somewhere we can always go back to, that welcomes us unconditionally. We love having a sanctuary that is in our more-or-less exclusive care and belongs to us in the deepest sense, as intimate to us as a family member.

We thrive when we know we have a safe, comforting, familiar place that holds us no matter what state we're in, and holds the few possessions this life lends us to nourish our bodies and our Souls. When we don't have this kind of sacred dwelling, we struggle. We can never fully rest or feel lasting freedom. A home gives us our lives a center of gravity, ground on which everything else can be built.

Our sense of home, however, isn't confined only to a literal house or apartment. Hopefully it extends to our neighborhood, town, region, continent, and planet. Hopefully it extends to our close relationships, community, and within our own selves, the bodies and Souls that contain us. Some people even feel at home in a car, in a tent, on the road. Wherever you can comfortably stay for the longest amount of time, there your home is. It is the hub of the wheel of your life.

But too much time at home becomes stifling. We humans are restless creatures, averse to being closed in, hungry to venture out, explore new places, and cultivate some familiarity there too. We seek out a variety of *havens* – spokes radiating out from our hub, refuges we can visit while we're out and about in the wider world.

These might be our favorite homes of our favorite people, parks or spots in Nature that speak to us, or places where our community gathers, like our workplace, school, faith community, or neighborhood cafe. When we have a network of these sacred waystations, it enlarges our sphere of identity and belonging. Here too we can rest for a while, before we head back home, or off further afield.

Many times in life, we all feel something – a call to adventure – beckoning us beyond the small world of our home, even beyond the medium world of our havens, out into the vast world of the unknown. Special places grab hold of our imagination and summon us on *pilgrimages* to visit them.

They may be far-flung cities or wildernesses, holy sites or cultural capitols, anywhere holding potent lessons for our lives. These are not places we stay very long or return to very often – they lie at the outer rim of our life, meant to remain largely unknown to us. And that's what makes them so alluring. There is always a cost of time and resources to go, sometimes a hefty one. Making such sacrifices and humbling ourselves before the mysteries of the world are how we honor these sacred journeys and destinations, how we treat them with the ceremony they deserve. And in return, they change us, turning the wheels of our lives in new directions.

So if these three things – home, havens, and pilgrimages – are what we need in terms of places in our lives, how would we describe the ways they've been impacted by the pandemic?

The Pandemic as Displacement

Firstly, COVID complicated or completely curtailed pilgrimages to far-away places for a while. In some ways, this was actually one of the silver linings of the pandemic.

We saw a drop in the CO_2 burden caused by air travel. And with so many places inaccessible, absence made the heart grow fonder: Many people developed a deeper appreciation for the destinations of potential pilgrimages, and for the global transportation network that helps us journey there. Plus, with a closing of international and urban voyages came an opening to domestic and natural ones – the Pandemic Era saw an uptick in camping, outdoor recreation in general, and "van-life." More people began seeking out the ceremonial realms of Nature and the nearby.[2]

These developments helped counteract the mental health crises exacerbated by the pandemic. This reinforced spiritual connectedness and environmentalism, in a time when life is increasingly mediated by electronics and the internet. We would do well to keep these trends going in the Recovery Era.

However, it was a whole different story for havens – here absence made for heartbreak. Leaving the nest to gather with friends, family, colleagues, or community was often out of the question, especially for people reliant

on public transportation. We could no longer linger at the institutions that normally provided us home away from home. Havens in Nature were about the only option, and not one available to everyone. We all experienced a prolonged dearth of variation in our spatial existence, a severe contracting of our little local worlds.

With the collapse of the spokes on most people's life-wheels, the hub of home was the only thing keeping the frame together. And while the expediencies that came with this may have been appealing at first, we soon realized that home cannot adequately hold everything for us.

It's not quite right to say our living spaces *became* our offices, classrooms, and community spaces – our homes did not in fact physically host all the people that make those havens what they are. Our homes became more like "windows" from which we looked in on our lives beyond. These "windows" were crowded not only by us personally, but crowded by everyone else living with us. Bedrooms and dining rooms hosted office gear, home offices hosted toys and classroom items. Meanwhile our offices, classrooms, and community spaces were dis-placed, dis-located into the ether, and subsumed in the virtual void we stared into from our "windows." And so these vistas felt not only cluttered, but cramped, down to the size of a computer monitor or a cellphone, sealed with a pane of glass.

Our modern technologies do indeed offer valuable *windows* into other places, but they are not *portals* that can magically transport us there, bodies and all. Although by interacting with a screen it may *feel* like we're accessing another spatial realm unto itself, we aren't: Cyberspace is not tactile and therefore not a *place* – our whole selves cannot go there.

Our bodies are an inextricable part of our identity and sense of place. When – while our minds are entranced with the view from some window – we forget for very long that our bodies exist, we do subtle, low-level damage to ourselves. By slowly losing touch with physicality we literally lose touch with reality. This is exactly what many people reported from the Pandemic Era everything-from-home paradigm.[3] Because it cannot hold our bodies, online is not a real place – let alone a home.

Furthermore, the fact that we can look through so many windows at so many different places *can* help expand our notion of home to encompass more of the globe, but this is a double-edged sword. As we saw with the phenomenon of "doom-scrolling," access to the bad news from every corner of the world can paralyze and frighten us. It can force us to turn inward on ourselves, dissociating from our kinship with humanity, all living beings, and the Earth. And especially when our bodies are meanwhile confined to a small space, we're prone to stew in this despair.

In short, it's hard for human beings – savanna-animals that we are – to stay sane while living in a window, let alone a crowded one, let alone one opening only to a filtered, fragmented, miniaturized, disembodied, overwhelming surreality. Trying to make a home in that kind of context can easily sap the essence of what home is supposed to be: a center of gravity rather than a collision of forces, a peaceful harbor amidst the storm of global turmoil, a place of rest and freedom. Thus the pandemic left us dislocated and displaced.

So how do we now re-locate? How do we find home and havens again, and pilgrimages?

What We Can Do: Location, Location, Location

When it comes to pilgrimages, we can keep up the good work:

> ➢ Focus on exploring more local and natural beauty, and on treating travel as a spiritual, ceremonial act.

This can also help us gain an expanded awareness of home and the possibilities for havens, mitigating the adverse mental health effects of the Pandemic Era.

In terms of havens, we may also need to continue what we're already doing:

> ➢ Finding new ones, reconnecting with old ones, and staying connected to any that have been significant to us in the last few years, especially those in Nature.

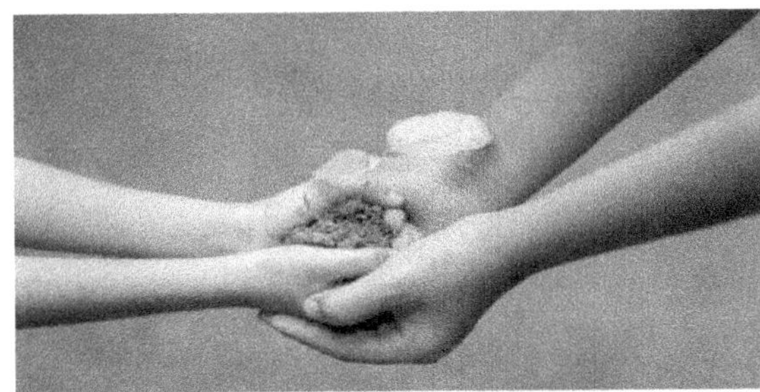

Since the coronavirus hit, most of us have been through a significant realignment in our social lives. We might now feel less attached to the same friends or community we did before, and uncertain of how to tend to those relationships going forward. We might be even less certain of where to find new havens on the other side of the pandemic. But for those of us who *do* have havens established:

> ➤ We need to invite folks who are currently adrift into our friend and community contexts, and welcome them in with hospitality.

We'll examine these questions more in Touchstone 9 on "village life," and you can read more about my recommended practices for building community on the InVocation blog: invitedinvocation.com/post/structure-spirituality-exercises-finding-community.[4]

As for our sense of home, after everything we discussed above it may seem like we have our work cut out for us. And we do – we need to resist the newly-normalized everything-from-home standard, and its repercussions from the past few years are a lot to recover from. But when we look at the tangible, day-to-day things we can each do to recover home and resist dislocation, our tasks are actually quite manageable:

> ➤ By returning to pilgrimages and havens, as well as to friends and community generally, we *broaden* our notion of home and relieve some of the pressure for it to somehow be all things.
>
> ➤ And by returning to our bodies, we *deepen* our perspective of home and relieve some of the pressure for *technology* to be all things.

As individuals and as a culture, it is physiologically, psychologically, and spiritually unhealthy for us to be so extremely online. For evidence, look no further than the effects the tech-saturated, Nature-deprived lifestyle is having on the mental health of young people.[5]

Our bodies offer drastically more fulfillment than most of what we do in front of a screen, and are even closer to us than the gadgets at our fingertips. Rather than limit our amazing physicality to the confines of furniture, air conditioning, slumped postures, and small glowing rectangles, we can instead limit technology.

> ➤ We can draw boundaries around the time that is available to electronically-mediated "life," and agree that the rest of our lives are for Life – real, living things.

Restraining news and entertainment are one thing, but it may be harder to swim against the tech-tide in community, education, our work-lives. However, the truth is unmistakable: socializing, learning, and working

predominantly via screens has always been worse for our mental and physical health than interacting with the real world of objects, people, and environment.[6]

Tech's flashiness, fun, and convenience in the 21st century economy are not good enough reasons to let it swallow our every activity. And these boons are definitively outweighed by the under-acknowledged harm (see Touchstone 9). This is especially true of social media. We lose creativity, productivity, and focus – Life – when we're treated as, and absorbed into, always-on machines.

Furthermore, the data from the Pandemic Era compels us to abandon the fully-virtual paradigm. While the research on remote work shows it's nice to have it as one option (again see Touchstone 9), it fails us as the only one. The data on remote schooling is even more conclusive: overall it was detrimental to learning, really only helpful as a stopgap and not as a substitute for the real deal.[7]

> ➢ For students to learn well, teachers to teach well, families to stay sane, and communities to cohere, most kids and adult learners must physically go to a classroom outside the home.

In summary, fully-online arrangements may seem efficient on their face, but are not efficient, nor human-friendly, in the long-run. Still, the hype about doing everything from home, not to mention about ceding more of ourselves to media and social media, will continue circulating in our cultural bloodstream. Our homes are the frontlines of this effort, and the places where it can actually be easiest and most effective.

> ➢ We have to stay inoculated against the hype, constraining tech rather than letting it constrain us.
>
> ➢ We can enforce hours during which screens are unavailable.
>
> ➢ We can keep devices covered, out of high traffic places, and off our person.
>
> ➢ If we must work from home, we can keep our office doors locked outside of hours, or otherwise maintain rituals that separate work time from other time (this is one of the benefits of having a work-site away from home and a commute on which to transition there).
>
> ➢ And all these measures can give us firmer footing as we advocate for humanity over technology in our workplaces, classrooms, and communities.

If we can take these bold steps, we'll restore our homes to places for restoration. We'll turn our living spaces from "windows" back to real sanctuaries, declutter them, and insulate them from the tyranny of a screened-in existence. We'll strengthen the integrity of the hubs that center us, so we can reconnect to havens and pilgrimages, spokes and rims, and bring balance to the wheel of our lives once more.

Reconnection: Restoring Relationships and Community

Nearly every person alive has endured profound upheavals in their social lives since the beginning of 2020.

In those early weeks, as communities and governments began to comprehend the enormity of the COVID health crisis, and as the subsequent cascade of restrictions took effect, we were all suddenly thrust into relative isolation. Soon we found ourselves overhauling our social lives: social-distancing, donning personal protective equipment, and migrating everything from board meetings to birthday parties into the virtual world. For some this seemed exciting or promising at first, but within a few months the costs to human health and happiness became clear.

In-person contact and conversation are basic needs, almost as essential as food and shelter. So when our circles of touch and talk shrank drastically, when our usually-overlapping lives fractured and diverged, it left us socially stunted.[8] People cannot learn or grow very well without each other. This is especially true of those who became most isolated – bereaved people, children, adolescents, elders, and people with many kinds of disabilities.

Loneliness reached pandemic proportions.[9] Something as fundamental to human existence as exposing our faces, voices, and hands to others suddenly became perilous. Now behind masks, screens, and windows, we all became more anonymous to one another. And even as we became physically insulated, we were now glued to our screens, news, and social media, mentally and emotionally exposed to constant reminders of the mounting trauma on all sides. So, without a critical mass of relationships surrounding us, we had to bear the weights of numbness, despair, sorrow – and fear – alone.

Many of us began to collapse in on ourselves. Some folks, additionally strained by the new demands of work, parenting, and caregiving, became too overwhelmed and burnt out to truly connect with anyone anymore. Some fell prey to depression and anxiety, drained of the ability to experience life as more than doom-scrolling. Some dissociated to cope, trying to hide from the news and tune out the pain, even turning to modes of escapism and addiction. Some got trapped in the echo chambers of their own minds or of an ideology, seeking someone to blame for their imprisonment, at worst descending into bitterness, paranoia, and animosity. Some found ways to share about their struggles with others and find healing; others did not, largely suffering in silence.

This all adds up to a great crisis of disconnection, a great rupture and rending in the fabric of belonging. More than anything else, this is what we need to recover from in the Recovery Era. More than anything else, this is the source of our grief, and where our passion is most needed. It's where we've lost the most, and yet now have the most to gain.

And this recovery is not something that will simply *happen*, without our conscious effort. As we covered in the Introduction, history shows that it is unwise to expect there will be a sudden, organic renewal of relationship and community after a global communal trauma. Now that the worst of the virus has passed and in-person gathering is back to pre-pandemic levels of safety, it can be tempting for us to assume the fabric of reconnection will simply re-weave itself.

Here's the problem: it won't. For evidence, all we need do is start by asking ourselves, "Do I feel true reconnection yet? Do most other people seem to?" My guess is our answers here do not inspire confidence in a laissez-faire attitude going forward.

Nor does the data advise us to outsource recovery. In the short-term, we're on track to be better off than in the worst of the pandemic, but certainly worse off than we were before COVID struck.[10] This is especially daunting news, given that our crisis of belonging preexists the Pandemic Era.[11] And in the long-term, as with all trauma, we need to be wary of underestimating the lingering consequences of this time of heightened crisis.

Relief is not the same thing as recovery, and cannot substitute for active repair. If we don't tend to them, the wounds inflicted on our social lives during this time are certain to fester and infect other parts of our lives. We need to set out to *do* the re-weaving, or it won't happen.

If we do nothing else to usher the Recovery Era along, we must restore relationships and community. So what does this look like?

Touchstone 8: Returning to Radical Presence

Let's Be Real

Have you ever been with a friend or someone else you love, and you're just in the moment with them, and vice versa? That's all radical presence is. You're simply in each other's company, concentrating on them, not thinking about other things, just *belonging* together.

We do this with other people all the time, and we *need* to. In Touchstones 6 and 7 we discussed how a sense of time and place, respectively, help us feel real. We can think of radical presence as stepping into the most important kind of time and place, one that necessitates its own category: being in the time and place that is a human being's focus of attention.

And just as much as our environment, this presence with another person is fundamental to knowing we're real. This is what we've learned from decades of studying mirror neurons and the formation of infants' brains.[12,13] Our relationships not only make us who we are, but *make us* in the most literal way. Nowhere else can we be reminded so poignantly that we matter and have an impact.

We also do this belonging with our own selves. If you've ever just journaled or meditated, or had to answer a deep question about your inner world, or just appreciated or contemplated your life for a minute, you've practiced radical presence with yourself, simulating mirror neurons. This is just as important a time and place, and just as foundational to our sense of being real. And you can also tap into radical presence via a task, whether related to work, play, creativity, learning, etc. Letting your attention become fully absorbed in any way, entering a flow-state or mindfulness of any kind, reminds us how substantial and alive we are.

How did the pandemic impact all of this? What's the opposite of radical presence? These questions have the same answer: distraction.

The Discontent of Distraction

Touchstones 6 and 7 also dealt with distraction. In Touchstone 6 we discussed the scattered attention that came with our disorientation in "COVID-time." And in Touchstone 7 we discussed how this has played out in the "everything-from-home" paradigm of technology substituting for real places, straining our focus. But in this Touchstone, we'll look more closely at the distractions inherent in relying on tech as we interface in our most intimate relationships – with family, friends, partners, and ourselves.

To stay in touch with many of our closest people during the pandemic, we were forced to rely on phone and video calling. Despite hopes that these would be a worthy substitute for face-to-face conversation, they didn't

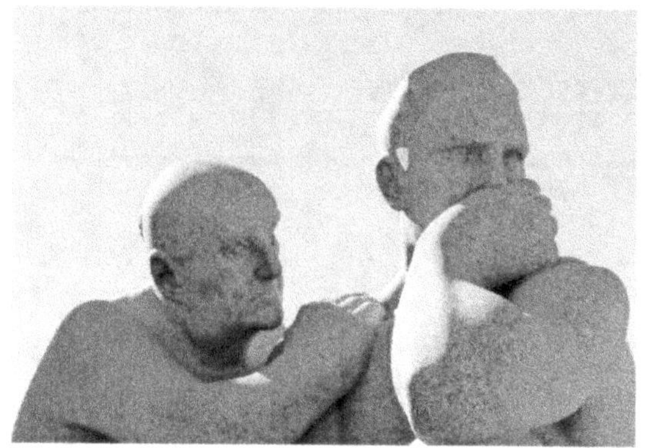

quite compare. People reported discontentedness with these forms of communication compared with in-person contact, and summarily drifted out of intimate relationship at a higher rate.[14,15]

Perhaps the biggest reason for this dissatisfaction is that phone and video calling doesn't work on mirror neurons nearly as well as in-person conversation.[16] To our bodies and brains, it simply doesn't feel as real or intimate to interact with someone via tech. These tools don't allow us to take in everything that comes with someone's holistic physical presence – touch, body language, minute facial expressions, voice inflection, breath, pheromones, and what we might call emotional vibes, or the subtle heat and electric charge we feel being next to a living person.

Nor does phone and video calling enable us to bond over a shared kinesthetic task, which is how so much of our relating happens. People on either end of a phone call can talk to each other while they each do tasks of their own, or while they're playing video games on the same server, but they can't do most other things they'd otherwise be doing together. Further, when we aren't doing the same task together in person, it's much easier for our independent tasks to become pure distraction. The bustle of chores on the other end of a call registers as noise and an averted gaze, rather than something that facilitates radical presence.

And then there's the distraction that comes with our devices themselves. It's all too easy to check texts, emails, social media, and more while someone is talking on a phone or video call. Yet we'd be careful not to do such a thing if the person was making a bid for our presence in-person – it would look like we were rudely ignoring them. Even if we aren't actively scrolling through our phones during a conversation, how often does the thought of awaiting notifications divert us from being in the moment? For most people, it's often – our concentration is high-jacked so frequently, we barely notice anymore.

Of course our devices infringe even more so on radical presence with *ourselves*. How often do any of us do 30 minutes of an uninterrupted, tech-less, contemplative activity anymore, whether reading, meditating, walking,

or simply sitting and thinking? What does it say about us that we eat, sleep, and go to the bathroom with these gadgets? What inner peace and internally-generated creativity do we lose out on from such distractedness? For evidence of the steep cost, we can look at the research on deterioration of our attention spans.[17] Or for even more of a wake-up-call, we can look at the impact that ubiquitous tech has on those who are both most distracted and have the most to lose from it: our young people.[18]

We can't blame this particular problem on COVID – we've been ceding attention to tech and losing touch with radical presence for many years. The pandemic just enabled and normalized tendencies we were already drifting into. But now we have a choice. We don't have to accept how much of our lives have been claimed by distraction.

So how do we reclaim radical presence with each other and with ourselves?

<u>Seizing the Moment, Closing the Social Distance</u>

As we covered under Touchstone 7, we need to resist the newly-normalized everything-from-home standard. We can also go a step further, and resist the devices-always-on-hand standard:

> ➤ We can practice silencing and stowing our devices more often, especially when we're in a conversation, taking time for solitude, or engaged in any other life-giving task.
>
> ➤ We can allocate a few dedicated minutes each hour to checking and responding to notifications, and otherwise turning them off, rather than always being available to them.
>
> ➤ We can even practice fasting or detoxing from tech for a whole day, morning, afternoon, or evening at a time.

But it isn't about simply depriving ourselves of devices. It's much more effective to actively give others the gift of radical presence:

> ➤ Each of us can be a ray of light amidst the gloom. In fact, you already have a beacon of light shining out from you at all times: your very own face. Your face is an undimmable source of beauty and life for the world around you, and the same goes for others' faces. If we can turn our luminous faces toward each other, we will heal the pain around us.
>
> ➤ We can practice mindfulness more often, simply being more attentive to the moment, our actions and interactions.
>
> ➤ A few things can help with this, like reciting a mantra, focusing on your breathing, or carrying a talisman – a small object you always keep in your pocket that reminds you to be intentional.

And the best training ground for being in the moment is always our own radical presence with ourselves:

> ➤ We can practice taking more time for stillness, silence, and reflection. I always recommend just starting with one stretch of 30 minutes during the workweek and another one on the weekend.

> ➤ This can take the form of meditation, prayer, journaling, or some other kind of gentle contemplative or spiritual practice, like going for a walk or reading a book.

> ➤ During these times, it can be helpful to reflect on the things in your life that really matter: the people you're connected to, simple pleasures, anything and anyone you're grateful for.

These are the things that most require your radical presence, and that will restore your feeling of being grounded, real, and peaceful.

Are your phone, computer, TV, etc. on this list of absolute, non-negotiable life essentials? My guess is, no. For almost all of us, they take too much and don't give enough in return. So let's put these devices in their place, at the periphery of our lives where they belong, rather than keeping them so central.

During the Pandemic Era, we had less say in how much we'd be distracted by our little glowing rectangles. But now we have a clear choice. Let's release the clutter infringing on our attention, and turn toward what matters with radical presence.

Touchstone 9: Returning to Village Life

Putting Tech to the Test

Decades before COVID-19, humanity began a strange experiment: seeing if we could replace work, learning, and recreation in intimate community – as we have practiced for millions of years – with work, learning, and recreation in relatively impersonal settings, via technology.

This experiment began with television, progressed to computers, video games, and the internet, and has culminated with smartphones, social media, and online offices, classrooms, and communities. In other words, we've been testing whether we could abandon the "village life" ingrained in our bodies, brains, genes, and societies in favor of an unprecedented "virtual life."

Proponents of the new virtual paradigm have predicted this would be a more fulfilling arrangement for everyone all around, putting forward at least four hypotheses that a tech-mediated social world would:

1. Reduce the "relational friction" that characterizes in-person interaction in work and schooling

2. Enable people to find a healthier balance between socializing and solitude

3. Increase the efficiency of labor

4. Prove to be "the same but better" at enabling communal connections compared to traditional village life

Then when the coronavirus hit in 2020, we had to restrict much of village life to preserve public health, but had the virtual world infrastructure to avoid a social standstill. Consequently, we were able to truly put the technologists' hypotheses to a full, all-encompassing trial as never before. With virtual life in extremis, we could now prove or disprove it as a viable alternative to village life.

So what were the results of this grand experiment? Let's see how the hypotheses above fared…

Relational Friction: Facts & Fictions

What is relational friction? To many people in the fields of economics, business, and technology, it means "inconvenient or time-wasting interpersonal interactions" or "obligatory socializing."

> A classic example is "water-cooler-talk" – happenstance conversations in an office environment, that at best seem to add little recognizable value to our work, and at worst actively distract from valuable working time.

> Another example is students' age-old love of talking to each other in and out of class, which is assumed by many to be an unqualified obstruction to learning.

These are examples of what virtual life, and what tech companies that promote and sell virtual life, promise to minimize or eliminate for us altogether.

And the pandemic seemed to offer a chance to make good on this promise once and for all.

> Now working from home, every office employee was finally forced to confine all their conversations to the business-only, goal-oriented venues of email and accompanying apps – finally, an efficient work environment!

> Now schooling from home, students could simply receive instruction and complete assignments, free from their peers' distractions – finally, an efficient learning environment!

Liberated from unnecessary chatting, how productive we would now be! Or so the theory went.

Of course, everyone on whom this theory was actually tested is already laughing at the how far off the mark it was.

> Despite the absence of water-cooler-talk, the number of meetings, workplace chatrooms, and time spent in these ballooned.[20]

> Without their peers, students from kindergarten to continuing education suffered immensely, in their studies as much as their social lives. And their stressed parents weren't ready to take on the interactive role usually filled by classmates.[21]

With these ineffective replacements for real village life, mental health declined across the board.[22] Why?

It turns out much, though not all, of our "unnecessary" chatting is really quite necessary.

> It alleviates our loneliness and isolation.

> It facilitates the bonding and belonging required for teamwork. It thereby propels the exchange of novel ideas and connections that drive innovation.

In short, a reasonable amount of friction is good for our jobs and certainly for our education.[23] Deep down, we know this to be true, and are hence wired for friction – so even when it's curtailed, we seek it out.

But what is a reasonable amount; how much is too much? At what point do unplanned conversations with others detract from the deeper, more intentional interactions our hearts long for? At what point does socializing cease to ease painful loneliness and begin infringing on generative solitude, the times we need for focused creativity and self-care? And does technology help us find a better interpersonal balance in this regard?

Balance?

First off, is there an optimal balance between socializing and solitude for human beings? Yes, though it varies from person-to-person.[24] Some people consistently prefer solitude and others socializing, thus we tend to skew introverted and extraverted respectively. These tendencies are stable throughout our lives, but not fixed – everyone has times of both introversion and extraversion, and the interplay between these fluctuates over time for each person. In all cases, when we get overwhelmed with socializing and "friction," we call it burnout, and when overwhelmed with solitude, we call it loneliness. Both sap our passion.

In general – and especially during the Pandemic Era experiment – virtual life has tended to exacerbate both burnout and loneliness. The benefits that technology contributes to socializing and solitude might not compensate proportionally for the damage.[25] It's true there are plenty of upsides to technology. But I've found that because it's so normalized and ubiquitous, we usually shy away from talking about the downsides.

As we move from the online-saturated Pandemic Era into the Recovery Era, now is an opportune time to give tech its due scrutiny.

Socializing & Burnout

Undeniably, modern technology enables an astounding breadth of social connections. The proliferation of computers, smartphones, the internet, and media makes it seem like the gamut of human experience is at our fingertips, along with the possibility for relationship with anyone on Earth.

But for every mile of relational breadth tech adds to our lives, it seems to rob a mile of relational *depth*, and gives us the impression that the social world is shallow, infinitely wide but only an inch deep.

> With the bombardments of social media, email, and online events and meetings, most of virtual relationality feels like a constant stream of mere fleeting glimpses into others' experiences. The stream only ever enlarges and intensifies, while the glimpses only become more ephemeral.

> And tragically, this leaves us feeling like the wild diversity of vocational, educational, and social life has somehow dissolved into a bland, tedious sameness.

These phenomena may be their own, more insidious types of relational friction.

To top it off, with our attention spans stretched too thin, cultivating real, deep relationship and community amidst all this becomes overwhelming. Thus, much of our *real*-world relational friction really does begin to feel more taxing, less like positive connectedness it truly is.

The pandemic only escalated all these tensions, to the point where people began burning out and withdrawing from work, school, and relational life in droves.[26] Hence what we covered in the Introduction: the Great Resignation, and the *Greater* Resignation.

<u>*Solitude & Loneliness*</u>

With all this strain to our extraversion, has virtual life at least compensated by enabling healthy introversion – solitude, and solitude without loneliness?

This too is one of the bold promises of tech: Every individual – now unfettered by relational friction, with every conceivable opportunity for creative self-expression, self-development, and self-directed labor and learning in the palm of their hand – can finally tap the true potential of their solitary consciousness; and as you do, you'll never have to feel alone, with like-minded folks a few clicks away. Unfortunately tech's reality hasn't quite lived up to these huge promises.

For one, the virtual world does not in fact offer as much or as varied opportunities for consciousness-growth as it claims to.

> Text, images, videos, and computational data are the "matter" – aka "content" – from which the virtual world is constructed, but are not *real matter*. As mere representation of actual things and events in the physical world, or ethereal pseudo-things and -events, "content" is fundamentally somewhat foreign to our flesh and blood bodies and minds.[27]

> "Content" tends to engage only a small bandwidth of our innate, multiple forms of human intelligence (verbal-linguistic and logical-mathematical) and does not directly empower, and can even interfere with, the rest (kinesthetic, naturalistic, etc.).[28] Even in the most interactive case of – a live video call between two people – the technology that facilitates the conversation also constitutes an obstruction to it.

In summary, it feels qualitatively different to connect with someone or something in the virtual world, and can leave us feeling more isolated and dislocated than real-world connection.

> Additionally, there is such a mind-numbing *amount* of content in cyberspace, such a staggering morass of information, that it requires immense time and concentration to sift through. This, as much as curiosity, is what sends us down virtual "rabbit holes" or scrolling feeds for hours. And this behavior is what tech companies exploit to keep us on their apps and siphon our time, money, and attention.

> When we do find something that sparks our curiosity, the medium through which we interact with it affects our experience. In the real world, all cognition is conversation, with others, with our environment, or just with ourselves. Or even with an author or artist – reading a great book feels like being in conversation. The virtual world operates more on a model of "performance" or "uploading" in the case of authors and influencers vying for our attention, and passive "spectatorship" or "downloading" in the case of everyone else.

Added up over time, these are lonely ways of exploring knowledge, and tend to foster a consumeristic dynamic: We take in far more content than we actually interact with.

Imbalance

There is even a relative solitariness to the process of making relationships virtually.

> To our brains – which are literally shaped from birth by touch and face-to-face contact – interacting with others through a screen, app, or mere text, images, and videos entails layers of separation, abstraction, and anonymity. It's no wonder online political discourse is so acrimonious, no wonder there's so much "ghosting" in online dating, so much cyberbullying and so many conspiracy theorist groups – it's easier to *other* others.[29]

Loneliness and the in-group-out-group dynamic feed each other. Just as virtual socializing tends to infringe on our solitude, it infringes on *healthy* socializing.[30]

Finally, all the above tends to foster alienation in our solitude, rather than replenishment:

> It is hard to be in true, generative solitude if you cannot be your full self – internally and externally connected in ways that are fundamental to being human. And it is usually harder to be your full self while plugged into the virtual world.[31]

> Not to mention, all this wading through the internet and social media, or doing anything virtual, has opportunity costs – it's time not spent in more fulfilling activities in the real world.

It's true that the annoying kind of relational friction – like boring small-talk with strangers or acquaintances – is alienating too. These shallow ways of socializing also carry opportunity costs, impinging on vital solitude and deep relationships, and in high doses, burning us out.[32] But most people are better at keeping their own healthy boundaries with friction in village life, than they are at staving off loneliness and burnout in virtual life.[33]

The Pandemic Era tech experiment demonstrated that virtual life tends to push introversion and extraversion to their extremes – toward burnout and loneliness – to everyone's detriment.

It's also true that relational friction carries opportunity costs in the workplace – too much water-cooler-talk is a drain on people's time and efficiency. And so technologists have hypothesized they can boost efficiency by doing away with the water cooler altogether and offering virtual offices. They seek to streamline the workday to a simple matter of small-talk-free toggling between apps, making the business environment truly business-only and therefore more productive. We can now look back on the pandemic to see the outcome of this part of the virtual-life experiment. How efficient is remote work?

Efficiency?

The data shows that even if productivity temporarily increased for people working from home at the very beginning of the pandemic, by now remote work productivity has slowed.[34] In fact, office productivity was already slowing long before 2020, a trend which has lasted, suspiciously, as long as social media has been in popular use.[35]

> So even if the data does indicate an efficiency spike in the short-term, the true test for remote work is staying power: Is the spike sustained? Unfortunately, no.[36]

> And for work on screens in general, it may never have been there in the first place.

To explain these phenomena, researchers cite the proliferation of perfunctory emails, the ease of workday distraction by media and social media, and other unnecessary cognitive strains.[37] Technology may indeed introduce just a different, less social, less productive *kind* of friction. This calls into question the very premise that the virtual world has really offered net productivity benefits, or even decreased relational friction.

> It may be that the whir of technology simply makes things *feel* faster and more productive than they actually are, and that tech corporations hype the illusion of efficiency because it's profitable rather than because it's true. It may be that we'd all be more productive if we didn't spend so much time in front of small, glowing rectangles. It may be that screens are only *easy*, not actually *efficient*.[38]

> And "relational friction" may merely be a euphemism for relationships and communal activities that don't obviously add to a tech company's quarterly earnings.

Such relationships and communal activities are what everything else – our whole society – is built on. Anti-friction technologists have mis-conceptualized human beings as atomized cogs in an economic machine, rather than seeing us as we really are – social, spiritual animals. They have underestimated how much of productivity and creativity at work are dependent on our ability to *learn*, and how much learning is dependent on our ability to socialize in-person.[39] A robust amount of friction makes the world go 'round.

The Same But Better?

This is even truer outside of work contexts, in the realm of raw relationship- and community-building. Here too COVID-19 presented a chance to prove whether technology could be a viable substitute for good-old-fashioned in-person socializing. Could video calls, online events, social media, and "the apps" be fulfilling replacements for village life in its most basic sense? Could virtual life offer equivalent venues for:

> ➢ communicating with loved ones,

> ➢ meeting potential friends and romantic partners, and

> ➢ generally sharing life with other people?

As we examine the technologists' final hypothesis – that virtual life is "the same but better" than village life – let's look more deeply at how technology impacts each of these social circles. Each one is like a concentric ring in our relational lives. We already addressed the dynamics around the inner ring, communicating with loved ones, in Touchstone 8 on radical presence. Now we'll focus on the middle and outer circles.

In general, we saw all of these rings curtailed during the pandemic tech experiment. We reported this contraction to be a painful experience, thrusting us into loneliness and isolation. It did not, as some speculated it might, improve our quality of life via "streamlining" our attention into fewer but deeper relationships. It wore away at our sense of passion rather than making more room for it.

These findings are more evidence supporting the case against migrating most of our social worlds online, and the case for returning to village life...

The Middle Ring: Potential Friends, Partners, & Acquaintances

To meet new people during the pandemic, we were forced to rely on video conferencing (for work and school friendships), "the apps" (for dating), and social media (in general). Of course, our increasing use of these was already in motion long before COVID, but suddenly it became the only option for most people. Again, these tools have largely failed as replacements for village-life milieus.

Without the ability to spend time with others predominantly in-person, the average number of new friends made in the last few years plummeted.[40] People also report more dissatisfaction with friendships mediated by video and social media, and difficulty making new friends now that these new norms are in place.[41,42] It seems

fulfilling friendships must, almost as a rule, be made face-to-face, and maintained that way to significant degree.

Additionally, now that in-person dating has fully resumed, but dating apps are still entrenched as the primary venue for potential partners to meet and begin courtship, we truly get to see how well online dating stacks up against village-life dating. It seems meeting via an app might not be as successful as meeting in school, work, and community contexts.[43] The reasons for this are complex, require much more research by social scientists, and will be explored in future articles on the InVocation blog!

The obvious but underestimated reason why village life is so much more effective at introducing us to new friends and partners is that it introduces us to *acquaintances*. In face-to-face contexts, we get to more and a wider variety of people, can more easily have spontaneous, surprising conversations with them.

And the dynamic of being among a crowd or group of people while these interactions are happening aids the process of one-on-one relationship-building. Most people feel greater permission to strike up a connection when others around them are doing the same. This is much less palpable in online settings, where every individual interacts from a disparate interface. Being clannish creatures, our instincts for romantic and platonic attraction are wired for village life, and the internet offers only paltry stand-ins.

The Outer Ring: Broader Community

To meet and connect with acquaintances during the pandemic, and participate in community in a broader sense, we were forced to rely on online events. Everything from faith services to community meetings, orientations to graduations was absorbed into the virtual world, which, again, proved it will not serve us well as the default social sphere.

Online events are most comparable to in-person ones in contexts that are meant for unidirectional communication, like a lecture or presentation. These at most require active listening from the audience. Unfortunately this is exactly the kind of event people are *least* interested in attending, whether virtually or in-person. Participants tune out of such events more quickly online than in the flesh, and retain less information from them in comparison.[44,45] This is compounded by the fact that in virtual events, participants are distracted as never before, able to work, scroll social media, join audio-only – or do all these at once – while a presenter is speaking.[46]

Besides, mere assimilation of "content," no matter how fascinating, is low on the list of reasons people attend an event in the first place; they could just read the article or watch the video.[47] Most often they go to participate in all the things that happen beyond being talked at. These include official agenda items like group discussions, but also the human sociality that happens off-script: mingling in the hallways, meeting up after the programming, whispering ideas and jokes while someone important is talking.

These things can't really happen to during online events, in part because participants can't control who or how many people they're interacting with in any given moment. (How many people have ever struck up a conversation in the chat with someone they didn't know, simply because their rectangles were next to each other on the screen? How many people have even been able to host their own makeshift video breakout room?)

It turns out the seemingly trivial relating we do in collective gatherings is not trivial at all. It is how we meet new acquaintances and therefore friends, colleagues, partners, and mentors. It is how we bathe ourselves in the awareness that society is – and strangers are – welcoming, dynamic, exciting, and full of possibility. This has huge implications for our mental health and social trust, without which nothing can function.

It Takes a Village

To sum up, let's look back at how the hypotheses of our Pandemic Era experiment with virtual life held up:

1. To the extent that tech reduces "relational friction," it also reduces other essential benefits that can only be gained from happenstance socializing.

2. Rather than helping us find balance, virtual life pushes us to the unhealthy extremes of socializing and solitude, breeding burnout and loneliness.

3. Tech decreases some of the efficiency of labor.

4. Virtual life is an all-around dissatisfying substitute for the activities of village life.

It's also worth noting that the results of the experiment turned out even worse for the people most harmed by the pandemic and most in need of social support: bereaved people, children, adolescents, elders, and people with many different kinds of disabilities.[48,49] For these folks especially – who together make up to the majority of the population – technology proved to be a staggering failure at enabling healthy solitude and socializing, alleviating loneliness and burnout, and helping maintain and grow circles of social support.

All of these clear results add up to a compelling conclusion: At best, virtual life can be a helpful fallback when village life is restricted, but it can never equate, and certainly should never be considered as a replacement. It's great as an option for socializing, solitude, work, school, and community, but is detrimental as a default.

Yet, tragically, instead of veering away from a technology, we seem to be driving our lives deeper into it. Every year we're only spending more time in front of screens. We're interfacing with computers and smartphones rather than corporeal human beings. We're spending our days in online offices, classrooms, and communities. We're spending our evenings with TV, video games, the internet, and social media rather than pursuing real recreation and creative hobbies.[31]

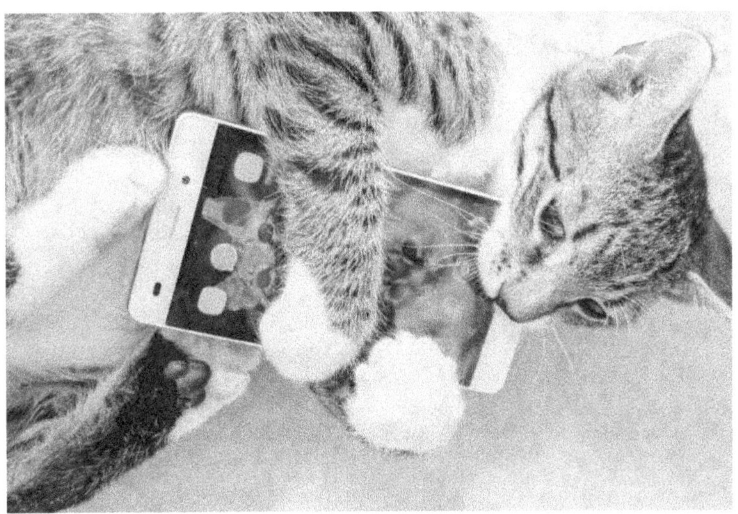

At what point will we accept that we're headed in the wrong direction, and wrest back our lives from the lure of tech? At what point will we choose healthy, Soul-nourishing, passion-filled village life over unhealthy, Soul-stifling, passion-scarce virtual "life?" At what point will we forsake the impersonal (im-personal – literally "person negating") and embrace the *in-personal?*

How about now? We've given tech its due, given virtual "life" the chance to show its true colors. The results are in: *the village life is the fulfilling life.*

So the choice is clear, but by no means easy. We *will* have to *choose.* We'll have to resist the siren's call of technology, fight our own inertia, disrupt the slide into ceding all of our magnificent human energy to little, colorful rectangles. We'll have to limit how much time and money we give to the corporations singing the siren's song, profiting off our burnout and loneliness and love of shiny new things. We'll have to regulate and boycott them and let their stock prices sag.

And we'll have to show up to real-world relationship and community again. We'll have to do the things we know are good for us:

> - Going into the office and classroom, and indulging small-talk and distractions
>
> - Meeting people known and unknown out at the wild frontiers of public places and community gatherings
>
> - Rediscovering the art of learning via books and conversations
>
> - Pulling the plug and urging our kids to go outside with their friends, and urging ourselves to go with them

We'll have to remember that despite the inconveniences of life off-screen, we really are happier and healthier and more passionate when we engage the world we were made for. We'll have to get our hands dirty and our bodies busy, renewing the messy, beautiful world of village life.

Touchstone 10: Centering the Margins

The three years of the Pandemic Era have been hard on everyone. But it's important for us to recognize they're been particularly hard on particular people.

Folks belonging to several demographic categories – and in our own lives, folks we know personally – have been hit harder by the coronavirus and its repercussions. There are communities and individuals who've been disregarded, overlooked, and underestimated in the recovery efforts so far. Likewise, there are parts of our own lives and selves that have been neglected.

With the individual struggles we've each gone through during this time – sometimes just to get through the day – and the collective struggle we've been in – sometimes just to cope with the most obvious emergencies caused by COVID – certain people and certain parts of ourselves that have needed recognition have instead been pushed to the margins.

And now that we're moving into the Recovery Era, it's time to give attention where it's due, bring the margins to the center of our awareness, and offer our compassion and camaraderie. This means doing some:

1. Soul-searching – learning more about where the Pandemic Era has taken the steepest toll, and what we can do about it – and

2. Soul-serving – directing our Recovery Era efforts to those places.

Soul-Searching & Soul-Serving: Pandemic Era Disparities

On which populations has the Pandemic Era taken the steepest toll? And what can be done about it? What does it look like to direct our Recovery Era efforts there?

First, how do we assess how steep the toll has been?[50] A few measures of data from the years since 2020 stand out – we can look at disparities in:[51]

I. COVID-related deaths: One reason to refer to these statistics is to inform us just how bad our Pandemic Era disparities are, according to our most heartbreaking metric. The other reason is that these numbers can help us recognize where we may need special space for grief and mourning.

2. Lingering consequences for access to basic necessities: Ongoing caregiving, educational, and employment struggles; food, healthcare, and housing insecurity; etc.[52]

3. Lingering consequences for mental health: Ongoing addiction, anxiety, depression, despair, grief, loneliness, stress, and rates of divorce, self-harm, suicide, etc.[53]

These data can guide us toward the issues on which we can concentrate our Recovery work.[54]

Then there are the demographics of people that have been hit hardest by these issues.[55] A few of these stand out as well – we can look at disparities in terms of:

1. Age – children, adolescents, and elders

2. Class or socioeconomic status – people experiencing poverty, incarceration, and homelessness

3. Disability status – people who need to interact with the medical system more often than the average person

4. Ethnicity and race – people of color, and Black and Indigenous people

5. Gender and sexuality – women, girls, and LGBTQI+ adults and youth

6. Nationality – people in dire circumstances abroad and in migration

7. Occupation – frontline or essential workers, and caregivers, including unpaid ones like parents

These data can tell us about the constituencies we should prioritize offering compassion and solidarity to.

It would be impossible to compile an exhaustive list of all the ways in which the pandemic has added to the marginalization of all these marginalized groups. Suffice it to say for now, the three issue categories above – COVID-related deaths, deprivation of basic necessities, and mental health struggles – have had an especially devastating impact on the above seven demographic categories. Despite the valiant efforts of researchers and journalists to collect data over the course of Pandemic Era, we have nothing remotely close to a synthesis: no accounting of all the many challenges the virus has posed, no proposal pinpointing where Recovery needs are most acute.[56] There are so many gaps in our understanding of what has happened and why, so many questions we may never fully answer and variables  we may never fully tease out. We'll be sorting through everything for years and decades to come.

In the meantime, the best we can do is simply highlight a few examples, hopefully sparking your imagination about where you can do some Soul-serving, taking action in your community.

Additionally, I believe it's worth asking – is there anything that connects all our post-pandemic problems and their solutions together, so it doesn't all feel so daunting and overwhelming?

I think there is. These are all problems of *isolation* – people are separated from what they need. And the thing that can connect them to what they need is the greatest need of all: relationship. The Recovery Era needs *connectors*, people like you and me, to reach out and build relationships, build a full, broad-based support system. So that's the lens through which I'll offer ideas for Soul-service...

Age disparities – children, adolescents, and elders

We've discussed in previous Touchstones how damaging isolation is for human beings. This is especially true for people whose brains and bodies need extra attention for growth and for maintenance. During the pandemic years, our kids lost much of their social worlds and learning progress.[57,58] So did our elders, many of whom additionally lost staggering numbers of their friends to the virus.[59]

These groups need to be enfolded into our circle of belonging once more. Now, you can:

➢ Volunteer as a mentor, coach, or tutor for local kids

➢ Volunteer at a senior center or long-term care facility

➢ Get to know the stories of the people you meet there

➢ Learn about and support relevant citizen advocacy and lobbying efforts

Class or socioeconomic status disparities – people experiencing poverty, incarceration, and homelessness

COVID-related illness, death, and other tragedies hit people on the socioeconomic margins with disproportionate force. And to make matters worse, there were barely any headlines about it. This just goes to show that few of us nurture connections with the folks in the most vulnerable kinds of situations.[60]

But we don't have to live in such isolation from each other. Now, you can:

➢ Volunteer your time, resources, and skills in mutual aid, a shelter, or a kitchen

➢ Volunteer at a prison or a program that helps people with criminal records get back on their feet

➢ Get to know the stories of the people you meet there

➢ Learn about and support relevant citizen advocacy and lobbying efforts

Disability status disparities – people who need to interact with the medical system and caregivers more often than the average person

Millions of people count on the healthcare system and supportive relationships to ensure they can live and thrive. But the threat of the coronavirus made it much harder, sometimes even impossible, for many of these folks to access the services they need. Then, for those living in long-term care facilities, there was the heightened threat of infection and death by COVID.

We need not leave people with disabilities isolated – we can create a society that honors their lives and presence rather than ignoring them.[61] Now, you can:

> Volunteer at a school or center that supports people with disabilities

> Get to know the stories of the people you meet there

> Learn about and support relevant citizen advocacy and lobbying efforts

Ethnicity and race disparities – people of color, and Black and Indigenous people

People in these communities are already underserved by the medical system, and yet are more likely to experience a medical emergency. Thus, as the virus both spread more quickly among them and also clogged up clinics, it precipitated an added health and health equity crisis. In addition, people of these communities were much more likely than white people to be laid off or take a pay cut during COVID, exacerbating financial stress; and students of color also suffered greater academic setbacks. Then appallingly, many people, giving into intolerance, used the fact that the virus originated in China as an excuse to persecute people of Chinese and Asian descent, leading to a rise in racist sentiment and hate crimes.[62]

In these ways and more, the Pandemic Era exposed the ongoing isolation imposed on various ethnic communities, as well as many of our other racial fault lines in America and internationally. The good news is that this also galvanized a movement of activists, led by people of color and Black and Indigenous people, to confront systemic racism more directly. We need to keep this momentum going, not letting it be a flash in the pan. Now, you can:

> Attend a training or class on racial justice, equity, diversity, and inclusion, or invite a trainer to host one for a community you're part of

> Get to know the stories of the people you meet there

> Learn about and support relevant citizen advocacy and lobbying efforts

Gender and sexuality disparities – women, girls, and LGBTQI+ adults and youth

These populations are also underserved by the health system, and are more likely than men, boys, and straight people to need routine and interventional sexual and reproductive care. Consequently, COVID caused them outsized health strains too, as well as outsized financial strains. Worse, social restrictions keeping them at home increased the likelihood they'd be subject to domestic violence, and that they'd have to risk homelessness and other consequences to escape.[63] Further, the support networks away from home that help mitigate these problems were curtailed.

These and many more issues kept women, girls, and LGBTQI+ people in even more precarious situations than they were in before the Pandemic Era.[64,65] Now, you can:

➢ Attend a training or class on gender and sexuality justice, equity, diversity, and inclusion, or invite a trainer to host one for a community you're part of

➢ Get to know the stories of the people you meet there

➢ Learn about and support relevant citizen advocacy and lobbying efforts

Nationality disparities – people in dire circumstances abroad and in migration

The U.S. as a country has experienced the highest total *number* of fatalities due to the coronavirus – over 1.1 million out of over 6.9 million worldwide.[66] But we aren't at the top of the list in terms of most deaths *relative* to population size – Peru has had the highest number per million people, twice the rate of the U.S.[67] And though the collateral damage of the virus has been destructive in our homeland, that's even more true in other places around the globe, many of which have had to cope with famines and other crises not found here.[68]

As the world's biggest economy and foremost superpower, our country has the greatest capacity to help in the Recovery effort. It's essential for us to consider how we can continue aiding people of other nations, as well as immigrants and refugees from them. And rather than just letting this be the job of government agencies and far-flung NGOs, every American can pitch in. Now, you can:

➢ Volunteer your time, resources, and skills for an international aid organization

➢ Get to know the stories of the people you meet there

➢ Learn about and support relevant citizen advocacy and lobbying efforts

Occupation disparities – frontline and essential workers, and caregivers,
including unpaid ones like parents

These folks have held the world together throughout the Pandemic Era, laboring with love and commitment every day. They've endured high COVID infection and mortality rates, severe burnout, PTSD, and other mental health crises. These hardships have fallen especially on the people of color who constitute a disproportionate number of essential frontline workers, adding to the challenges already noted above. And they've fallen on the

women who make up the majority of employees in care-work (education, healthcare, etc.), as well as the majority of active parents and caregivers, again on top of everything else.[69,70,71,72]

After all of *their* valiant, underappreciated Soul-serving, it's time these folks get the recognition, rest, and working conditions they've deserved and needed this whole time. Let's offer them some Soul-service as a token of our gratitude. Now, you can:

> Donate meals and money to workers and caregivers in your local area

> Get to know the stories of the people you meet there

> Learn about and support relevant citizen advocacy and lobbying efforts

These are just a few examples of what to watch for in the aftermath of COVID, and just a few of the ways we can extend compassion and solidarity to those who've been on the margins. May we prioritize these places that most need recovery as we advance into the Recovery Era.

Soul-Searching & Soul-Serving: The Margins in Our Lives

Where has the Pandemic Era taken the steepest toll on people we know, and on ourselves? And what can we and they do about it? What does it look like to direct our Recovery Era efforts there?

Whether or not we personally know people from all the demographic categories above, we all know people who've been acutely or persistently affected by the pandemic and its collateral damage. Hopefully they're getting the help they need, but if not, they may be someone who could use your compassion and camaraderie, for whom we can do some Soul-serving.

> Who are these people in your life?

> What are they struggling with?

> What's helping or could help with that? These could be solutions identified above, or something you do for them or invite them into. Who else can help?

> What's been neglected that would enliven them again?

And whether or not *you personally* fall into one of the demographic categories above, whether or not you especially continue to struggle in the aftermath of the pandemic, there very well may be an important part of *your* life that's been pushed to the margins. In my work and conversations since 2020, a common theme I've noticed is the need to reignite *passion* – that vitality, vivacity, vigor, and verve – again.

For many of us, the pandemic has been draining on our ability to be as playful and creative and active as we want to be in our lives, sapped us of an animating sense of meaning in our work. In most cases, we've just been

getting by these last few years, trying to hold onto what energy we have, trying not to stall out. With everything so uncertain, it's been hard to muster an awareness of possibility in our work, education, recreation, and relationships. With our worlds feeling smaller than we're used to, it's been tough to remember life can be an adventure.

COVID has clipped many people's wings. But our wings can heal, and we can spread them again. You too deserve compassion and camaraderie, including from yourself.

> What are you struggling with?

> What's helping or could help with that? These could be solutions identified above, or something else entirely. Who else can help?

> What's been neglected that would enliven you again?

If you're seeking to ignite more passion in your life, I've found that chances are, engaging in some form of Soul-service might be just what does the trick. And if you feel you have little to give, I'd say you're severely underestimating yourself. Just about every kind of volunteering, activism, and mentorship is sorely needed, and is as deeply appreciated as it is gratifying. You'd be surprised how much good can come from you just showing up, and how much energy and satisfaction you'll get from it in return.

Additionally, I encourage you to subscribe to the InVocation blog to stay tuned for updates on my upcoming course, *Soul Sagas: Finding Our True Callings in Our Life Stories*. This class is all about discovering and following your deepest passions, which in itself is a form of Soul-service: We need people living lives of purpose and contribution, now more than ever.

I sincerely hope this and all the other Touchstones have helped as you search your own Soul. I hope they've helped you identify which parts of your experience from the Pandemic Era have been pushed to the sidelines, and helped you identify the same for others. And I sincerely hope these Lessons from the Pandemic have shown you how to bring those margins to the center of your attention, so you and those you love can truly find healing, catharsis, and support.

I hope my Recovery Era effort here has served your Soul, and that as you share it with others, it can serve many more Souls. I hope you go forth, Soul-serving everyone you can.

A Blessing

May you know my gratitude to you, for joining me on this journey.

May you face the uncertain future with resilient hope and steadfast courage. May you invite others to do the same.

May you enlist in the Greater Reengagement and Reimagination, in the Recovery Era, and in the Passionate Era beyond. May you invite others to do the same.

May you use what you've learned here as a Transitional Ceremony for yourself. May you help us move through our pain. May you invite others to do the same.

May you know comfort in your grief. May you know that those you've lost have not lost you. May you know the great gaze of love watches over you, always.

May you love this life with all that you have within you. And may life bless you with all its wild wonders.

Onward.

TOUCHSTONE 1
STORYTELLING

TOUCHSTONE 2
BEING IN NATURE

TOUCHSTONE 3
CREATIVE PROJECTS

TOUCHSTONE 4
EULOGIZING

TOUCHSTONE 5
INTENTION-SETTING

TOUCHSTONE 6
SACRED TIMES

TOUCHSTONE 7
SACRED PLACES

TOUCHSTONE 8
RADICAL PRESENCE

TOUCHSTONE 9
VILLAGE LIFE

TOUCHSTONE 10
THE MARGINS

Works Cited, Further Reading

INTRODUCTION

1. Hewlett, E., Takino, S., Nishina , Y., & Prinz, C. (2021, May 12). *Tackling the mental health impact of the COVID-19 crisis: An integrated, whole-of-society response*. OECD. https://www.oecd.org/coronavirus/policy-responses/tackling-the-mental-health-impact-of-the-covid-19-crisis-an-integrated-whole-of-society-response-0ccafa0b/

2. Patulny, R., & Bower, M. (2022, June 23). *Beware the "loneliness gap"? Examining emerging inequalities and long-term risks of loneliness and isolation emerging from COVID-19*. Wiley Online Library. https://doi.org/10.1002/ajs4.223

3. Davis, S. (2022, July 12). *59% of U.S. adults find it harder to form relationships since covid-19, survey reveals - here's how that can harm your health*. Forbes. https://www.forbes.com/health/mind/social-anxiety-since-covid-survey/

4. Pasquini, G., & Keeter, S. (2022, December 12). *At least four-in-ten U.S. adults have faced high levels of psychological distress during COVID-19 pandemic*. Pew Research Center. https://www.pewresearch.org/fact-tank/2022/12/12/at-least-four-in-ten-u-s-adults-have-faced-high-levels-of-psychological-distress-during-covid-19-pandemic/

5. Clifton, J. (2021, December 3). *The next global pandemic: Mental health*. Gallup.com. https://www.gallup.com/workplace/357710/next-global-pandemic-mental-health.aspx

6. Parker, K., & Horowitz, J. M. (2022, March 9). *Majority of workers who quit a job in 2021 cite low pay, no opportunities for advancement, feeling disrespected*. Pew Research Center. https://www.pewresearch.org/fact-tank/2022/03/09/majority-of-workers-who-quit-a-job-in-2021-cite-low-pay-no-opportunities-for-advancement-feeling-disrespected/

7. Johnson, C. (n.d.). *Our team*. The Milkweed Group. http://milkweedgroup.com/about-us/our-team/

8. Keeter, S. (2021, March 16). *Many Americans continue to experience mental health difficulties as pandemic enters second year*. Pew Research Center. https://www.pewresearch.org/fact-tank/2021/03/16/many-americans-continue-to-experience-mental-health-difficulties-as-pandemic-enters-second-year/

9. World Health Organization. (2022, March 2). *Covid-19 pandemic triggers 25% increase in prevalence of anxiety and depression worldwide*. World Health Organization. https://www.who.int/news/item/02-03-2022-covid-19-pandemic-triggers-25-increase-in-prevalence-of-anxiety-and-depression-worldwide

10. Putnam, R. D., & Garrett, S. R. (2020). *The upswing: How America came together a century ago and how we can do it again*. Simon & Schuster.

11. Kochhar, R., & Sechopoulos, S. (2022, April 20). *Covid-19 pandemic pinches finances of America's lower- and middle-income families*. Pew Research Center's Social & Demographic Trends Project. https://www.pewresearch.org/social-trends/2022/04/20/covid-19-pandemic-pinches-finances-of-americas-lower-and-middle-income-families/

12. Committee, U. S. J. E. (2019, September 5). *Long-term trends in deaths of despair*. United States Joint Economic Committee. https://www.jec.senate.gov/public/index.cfm/republicans/2019/9/long-term-trends-in-deaths-of-despair

13. Wikimedia Foundation. (2023, March 23). *Bo Burnham: Inside*. Wikipedia. https://en.wikipedia.org/wiki/Bo_Burnham:_Inside

14. Wikimedia Foundation. (2023, March 20). *Spanish flu*. Wikipedia. https://en.wikipedia.org/wiki/Spanish_flu

15. Wikimedia Foundation. (2023, March 21). *World War I*. Wikipedia. https://en.wikipedia.org/wiki/World_War_I

16. Wikimedia Foundation. (2023, March 22). *Treaty of versailles*. Wikipedia. https://en.wikipedia.org/wiki/Treaty_of_Versailles

17. Wikimedia Foundation. (2023, March 16). *Paris peace conference (1919–1920)*. Wikipedia. https://en.wikipedia.org/wiki/Paris_Peace_Conference_(1919%E2%80%931920)

18. Wikimedia Foundation. (2023, February 6). *Blockade of Germany*. Wikipedia. https://en.wikipedia.org/wiki/Blockade_of_Germany

19. Wikimedia Foundation. (2023, February 19). *Article 231 of the Treaty of Versailles*. Wikipedia. https://en.wikipedia.org/wiki/Article_231_of_the_Treaty_of_Versailles

20. Wikimedia Foundation. (2023, March 16). *Aftermath of World War I*. Wikipedia.
      https://en.wikipedia.org/wiki/Aftermath_of_World_War_I

21. Wikimedia Foundation. (2023, March 16). *World War I reparations*. Wikipedia.
      https://en.wikipedia.org/wiki/World_War_I_reparations

22. *Recovery Series News, research and analysis*. The Conversation. (2020, July 28).
      https://theconversation.com/uk/topics/recovery-series-87523

23. Wikimedia Foundation. (2023, March 20). *Roaring twenties*. Wikipedia. https://en.wikipedia.org/wiki/Roaring_Twenties

24. Wikimedia Foundation. (2023, March 19). *Lost generation*. Wikipedia. https://en.wikipedia.org/wiki/Lost_Generation

25. Wikimedia Foundation. (2023, March 22). *Marshall Plan*. Wikipedia. https://en.wikipedia.org/wiki/Marshall_Plan

26. Wikimedia Foundation. (2023, March 21). *The Blitz*. Wikipedia. https://en.wikipedia.org/wiki/The_Blitz

27. Bregman, R. (2020). *Humankind: A hopeful history*. (E. Manton & E. Moore, Trans.). Little, Brown and Company.

28. Solnit, R. (2020). *A paradise built in hell: The extraordinary communities that arise in disaster*. Penguin Books.

29. Bard, B. (2023, March 21). *Guide for the Grief Journey: Ten Touchstones*. InVocation. https://invitedinvocation.com/grief-journey-guide

IMAGE CREDITS

1.   https://unsplash.com/photos/LkDeIpV2k-I - cover image

2.   https://pixabay.com/photos/compass-map-direction-degrees-2946959/ - cover image

3.   https://pixabay.com/photos/sign-road-warning-signpost-749470/

4.   https://pixabay.com/photos/people-crowd-hands-clapping-party-2607201/ - cover image

5.   https://pixabay.com/photos/signpost-direction-directions-sign-4312750/ - cover image

6.   https://unsplash.com/photos/5QvsDOAaXPk

7.   https://pixabay.com/photos/road-sign-asphalt-road-sign-90390/

8.   https://commons.wikimedia.org/wiki/File:Connecticut_National_Guard_sets_up_federal_medical_station_equipment_at_Southern_Connecticut_State_University_%288%29.jpg

9.   https://commons.wikimedia.org/wiki/File:Camp_Funston%2C_at_Fort_Riley%2C_Kansas%2C_during_the_1918_Spanish_flu_pandemic.jpg

10. https://commons.wikimedia.org/wiki/File:Hitler_accepts_the_ovation_of_the_Reichstag_after_announcing_an_Anschluss_with_Austria%2C_Berlin%2C_March_1938.jpg

11. https://commons.wikimedia.org/wiki/File:Paris_Greets_Its_Liberators_-_DPLA_-_afbd076e65bc0497100087ea1749d52c.jpg

12. https://commons.wikimedia.org/wiki/File:Verwoestingen_na_luchtaanval_op_Londen._Puinruimen%2C_Bestanddeelnr_935-3516.jpg

13. https://commons.wikimedia.org/wiki/File:Konrad-Adenauer-Bruecke.jpg

14. https://pixabay.com/photos/cementerio-flor-cemetery-death-948048/

15. https://commons.wikimedia.org/wiki/File:Samantha_Power_visited_the_COVID_memorial_at_the_National_Mall_%281%29.jpg

16. https://commons.wikimedia.org/wiki/File:US_Congress_moment_of_silence_for_COVID-19_victims%2C_Washington%2C_D.C._%282021-02-23%29.jpg

PART 1

1. Bard, B. (2023, March 21). *Guide for the Grief Journey: Ten Touchstones*. InVocation. https://invitedinvocation.com/grief-journey-guide

2. Bard, B. (2022, January 2). *Moving through existential despair to resilient hope*. InVocation. https://invitedinvocation.com/post/existential-despair-hope-mystic-spirituality

3. Bard, B. (2022, January 21). *What is spirituality? why do we need it? - part 1*. InVocation. https://invitedinvocation.com/post/what-is-spirituality-religion-definition

4. Bard, B. (2022, January 5). *Simple settings for spiritual growth – part 1: Nature & ritual*. InVocation. https://invitedinvocation.com/post/spiritual-growth-tools-nature-practices

5. Bard, B. (2022, January 3). *Simple settings for spiritual growth – part 3: grief, calling, & vocation*. InVocation. https://invitedinvocation.com/post/spiritual-growth-grief-calling-vocation

6. Bard, B. (2023, March 21). *Guide for the Grief Journey: Ten Touchstones*. InVocation. https://invitedinvocation.com/grief-journey-guide

IMAGE CREDITS

1. https://upload.wikimedia.org/wikipedia/commons/thumb/c/cf/Covid-Vaccine-67_%2850753109591%29.jpg/640px-Covid-Vaccine-67_%2850753109591%29.jpg

2. https://pixabay.com/photos/bonfire-people-night-group-6953273/

3. https://pixabay.com/photos/lamp-flame-clear-lighting-lit-1106981/ - cover image

4. Rick Beckel

5. Rick Beckel

6. Rick Beckel

7. Rick Beckel

8. https://pixabay.com/photos/broken-glass-sun-clouds-shattered-549087/

9. https://pixabay.com/photos/crystal-ball-tree-sunrise-morning-6134758/ - cover image

10. https://pixabay.com/photos/sunflower-faded-nature-blossom-4504059/

11. https://pixabay.com/photos/sunflower-bud-flower-yellow-flower-3564207/

12. https://pixabay.com/photos/sunflowers-flowers-sun-yellow-7353922/

13. https://pixabay.com/photos/sunflowers-field-sunset-sun-6007847/ - cover image

14. https://pixabay.com/photos/beach-flag-beach-sea-flag-ocean-7196035/ - cover image

15. https://pixabay.com/photos/kite-beach-sky-air-colors-sun-4201894/

PART 2

1. Bard, B. (2022, February 8). *Simple structure for your spirituality – part 2: Exercises for finding consistency.* InVocation. https://www.invitedinvocation.com/post/structure-spirituality-exercises-finding-consistency

2. *2022 outdoor participation trends report.* Outdoor Industry Association. (2022, September 19). https://outdoorindustry.org/resource/2022-outdoor-participation-trends-report/

3. Ciaunica, A., McEllin, L., Kiverstein, J., Gallese, V., Hohwy, J., & Woźniak, M. (2022). Zoomed out: Digital Media use and depersonalization experiences during the COVID-19 lockdown. *Scientific Reports, 12.* https://doi.org/10.1038/s41598-022-07657-8

4. Bard, B. (2022, February 11). *Simple structure for your spirituality – part 3: Exercises for finding community.* InVocation. https://www.invitedinvocation.com/post/structure-spirituality-exercises-finding-community

5. Twenge, J. M., & Campbell, W. K. (2018). Associations between screen time and lower psychological well-being among children and adolescents: Evidence from a population-based study. *Preventive Medicine Reports, 12,* 271–283. ScienceDirect. https://doi.org/10.1016/j.pmedr.2018.10.003

6. Park, J. H., Moon, J. H., Kim, H. J., Kong, M. H., & Oh, Y. H. (2020). Sedentary lifestyle: Overview of updated evidence of potential health risks. *Korean Journal of Family Medicine, 41*(6), 365–373. https://doi.org/10.4082/kjfm.20.0165

7. Anderson, M., Faverio, M., & McClain, C. (2022, June 2). *How teens navigate school during covid-19.* Pew Research Center: Internet, Science & Tech. https://www.pewresearch.org/internet/2022/06/02/how-teens-navigate-school-during-covid-19/

8. Pasquini, G., & Keeter, S. (2022, December 12). *At least four-in-ten U.S. adults have faced high levels of psychological distress during COVID-19 pandemic.* Pew Research Center. https://www.pewresearch.org/fact-tank/2022/12/12/at-least-four-in-ten-u-s-adults-have-faced-high-levels-of-psychological-distress-during-covid-19-pandemic/

9. Ernst, M., Niederer, D., Werner, A. M., Czaja, S. J., Mikton, C., Ong, A. D., Rosen, T., Brähler, E., & Beutel, M. E. (2022). Loneliness before and during the COVID-19 pandemic: A systematic review with meta-analysis. *American Psychologist, 77*(5), 660–677. https://doi.org/10.1037/amp0001005

10. Hewlett, E., Takino, S., Nishina , Y., & Prinz, C. (2021, May 12). *Tackling the mental health impact of the COVID-19 crisis: An integrated, whole-of-society response.* OECD. https://www.oecd.org/coronavirus/policy-responses/tackling-the-mental-health-impact-of-the-covid-19-crisis-an-integrated-whole-of-society-response-0ccafa0b/

11. McCormack, W. (2020, September 17). *From I to we.* The New Republic. https://newrepublic.com/article/159276/the-upswing-book-review-robert-putnam-shaylyn-romney-garrett

12. Wikimedia Foundation. (2023, March 7). *Mirror neuron.* Wikipedia. https://en.wikipedia.org/wiki/Mirror_neuron

13. Rayson, H., Bonaiuto, J. J., Ferrari, P. F., & Murray, L. (2017, September 15). *Early maternal mirroring predicts infant motor system activation during facial expression observation.* Nature. https://doi.org/10.1038/s41598-017-12097-w

14. Lippke, S., Fischer, M. A., & Ratz, T. (2021, January 12). *Physical activity, loneliness, and meaning of friendship in young individuals – a mixed-methods investigation prior to and during the COVID-19 pandemic with three cross-sectional studies.* Frontiers. https://doi.org/10.3389/fpsyg.2021.617267

15. Patulny, R., & Bower, M. (2022, June 23). *Beware the "loneliness gap"? Examining emerging inequalities and long-term risks of loneliness and isolation emerging from COVID-19.* Wiley Online Library. https://doi.org/10.1002/ajs4.223

16. Isabella, G., & Carvalho, H. C. (2016). Emotional contagion and socialization: reflection on virtual interaction. *Emotions, Technology, and Behaviors,* 63–82. https://doi.org/10.1016/b978-0-12-801873-6.00004-2

17. MacKay, J. (2018, October 17). *Communication overload: Most workers can't go 6 minutes without checking email.* RescueTime Blog. https://blog.rescuetime.com/communication-multitasking-switches/

18. Twenge, J. M. (2018). iGen why today's super-connected kids are growing up less rebellious, more tolerant, less happy-and completely unprepared for adulthood*: *(and what this means for the rest of us). Atria Paperback.

19. Ruth , K., Igielnik, R., & Horowitz, J. (2020, December 9). *How the coronavirus outbreak has – and hasn't – changed the way Americans work.* Pew Research Center's Social & Demographic Trends Project. https://www.pewresearch.org/social-trends/2020/12/09/how-the-coronavirus-outbreak-has-and-hasnt-changed-the-way-americans-work/

20. Anderson, M., McClain, C., & Faverio, M. (2022, June 2). *How teens navigate school during covid-19.* Pew Research Center: Internet, Science & Tech. https://www.pewresearch.org/internet/2022/06/02/how-teens-navigate-school-during-covid-19/

21. Clair, R., Gordon, M., Kroon, M., & Reilly, C. (2021). The effects of social isolation on well-being and life satisfaction during pandemic. *Humanities and Social Sciences Communications, 8.* https://doi.org/10.1057/s41599-021-00710-3

22. Kulcar, V., Bork-Hüffer, T., & Schneider, A.-M. (2022). Getting through the crisis together: Do friendships contribute to university students' resilience during the COVID-19 pandemic? *Frontiers in Psychology, 13.* https://doi.org/10.3389/fpsyg.2022.880646

23. Luo, P., LaPalme, M. L., Cipriano, C., & Brackett, M. A. (2022). The association between sociability and covid-19 pandemic stress. *Frontiers in Psychology, 13.* https://doi.org/10.3389/fpsyg.2022.828076

24. Jones, S. E., Ethier, K. A., Hertz, M., DeGue, S., Le, V. D., Thornton, J., Lim, C., Dittus, P. J., & Geda, S. (2022). Mental health, suicidality, and connectedness among high school students during the COVID-19 pandemic — adolescent behaviors and experiences survey, United States, January–June 2021. *MMWR Supplements, 71*(3), 16–21. https://doi.org/10.15585/mmwr.su7103a3

25. McClain, C., Vogels, E. A., Perrin, A., Sechopoulos, S., & Rainie, L. (2021, September 1). *The internet and the pandemic.* Pew Research Center: Internet, Science & Tech. https://www.pewresearch.org/internet/2021/09/01/the-internet-and-the-pandemic/

26. Ciaunica, A., McEllin, L., Kiverstein, J., Gallese, V., Hohwy, J., & Woźniak, M. (2022). Zoomed out: Digital Media use and depersonalization experiences during the COVID-19 lockdown. *Scientific Reports, 12.* https://doi.org/10.1038/s41598-022-07657-8

27. Wikimedia Foundation. (2023, March 21). *Theory of multiple intelligences.* Wikipedia. https://en.wikipedia.org/wiki/Theory_of_multiple_intelligences

28. Doherty, C., Kiley, J., & Oliphant, B. (2022, August 9). *As partisan hostility grows, signs of frustration with the two-Party system.* Pew Research Center - U.S. Politics & Policy. https://www.pewresearch.org/politics/2022/08/09/as-partisan-hostility-grows-signs-of-frustration-with-the-two-party-system/

29. Auxier, B. (2020, October 15). *64% of Americans say social media have a mostly negative effect on the way things are going in the U.S. Today.* Pew Research Center. https://www.pewresearch.org/fact-tank/2020/10/15/64-of-americans-say-social-media-have-a-mostly-negative-effect-on-the-way-things-are-going-in-the-u-s-today/

30. Anderson, M., Vogels, E. A., Perrin, A., & Rainie, L. (2022, November 16). *Connection, creativity and drama: Teen life on social media in 2022.* Pew Research Center: Internet, Science & Tech. https://www.pewresearch.org/internet/2022/11/16/connection-creativity-and-drama-teen-life-on-social-media-in-2022/

31. Vogels, E. A., Gelles-Watnick, R., & Massarat, N. (2022, August 10). *Teens, social media and technology 2022.* Pew Research Center: Internet, Science & Tech. https://www.pewresearch.org/internet/2022/08/10/teens-social-media-and-technology-2022/

32. Edwards , E., & Fox, M. (2018, September 10). *More teens addicted to social media, prefer texting to talking.* NBCNews. https://www.nbcnews.com/health/health-news/more-teens-addicted-social-media-say-they-re-wise-distractions-n908126

33. Escudero, C., & Kleinman, M. (2022, December 19). *The shift to working from home: How has it affected productivity?* Economics Observatory. https://www.economicsobservatory.com/the-shift-to-working-from-home-how-has-it-affected-productivity

34. *Long-term labor productivity in the nonfarm business sector since 1947.* U.S. Bureau of Labor Statistics. (2023, March 2). https://www.bls.gov/productivity/graphics/2022/graphic-1.htm

35. Parker, K., Horowitz, J., & Minkin, R. (2022, February 16). *Covid-19 pandemic continues to reshape work in America.* Pew Research Center's Social & Demographic Trends Project. https://www.pewresearch.org/social-trends/2022/02/16/covid-19-pandemic-continues-to-reshape-work-in-america/

36. MacKay, J. (2018, May 29). *Interruptions at work are killing your focus, productivity, and motivation.* RescueTime Blog. https://blog.rescuetime.com/interruptions-at-work/

37. MacKay, J. (2018, October 17). *Communication overload: Most workers can't go 6 minutes without checking email.* RescueTime Blog. https://blog.rescuetime.com/communication-multitasking-switches/

38. Harter, J. (2022, April 25). *U.S. employee engagement slump continues.* Gallup. https://www.gallup.com/workplace/391922/employee-engagement-slump-continues.aspx

39. Patulny, R., & Bower, M. (2022, June 23). *Beware the "loneliness gap"? Examining emerging inequalities and long-term risks of loneliness and isolation emerging from COVID-19.* Wiley Online Library. https://doi.org/10.1002/ajs4.223

40. Lippke, S., Fischer, M. A., & Ratz, T. (2021, January 12). *Physical activity, loneliness, and meaning of friendship in young individuals – a mixed-methods investigation prior to and during the COVID-19 pandemic with three cross-sectional studies.* Frontiers. https://doi.org/10.3389/fpsyg.2021.617267

41. Davis, S. (2022, July 12). *59% of U.S. adults find it harder to form relationships since covid-19, survey reveals - here's how that can harm your health.* Forbes. https://www.forbes.com/health/mind/social-anxiety-since-covid-survey/

42. Anderson, M., Vogels, E. A., & Turner, E. (2023, February 6). *The virtues and downsides of online dating*. Pew Research Center: Internet, Science & Tech. https://www.pewresearch.org/internet/2020/02/06/the-virtues-and-downsides-of-online-dating/

43. Loeb, S. (2020, March 20). *How effective is online learning? what the research does and doesn't tell us (opinion)*. Education Week. https://www.edweek.org/technology/opinion-how-effective-is-online-learning-what-the-research-does-and-doesnt-tell-us/2020/03

44. Cellini, S. R. (2021, August 13). *How does virtual learning impact students in higher education?* Brookings. https://www.brookings.edu/blog/brown-center-chalkboard/2021/08/13/how-does-virtual-learning-impact-students-in-higher-education/

45. Nguyen, T., Netto, C. L., Wilkins, J. F., Bröker, P., Vargas, E. E., Sealfon, C. D., Puthipiroj, P., Li, K. S., Bowler, J. E., Hinson, H. R., Pujar, M., & Stein, G. M. (2021). Insights into students' experiences and perceptions of remote learning methods: From the COVID-19 pandemic to best practice for the future. *Frontiers in Education, 6*. https://doi.org/10.3389/feduc.2021.647986

46. Bawa, P. (2016). Retention in online courses: Exploring issues and solutions - a literature review. *SAGE Open, 6*(1). https://doi.org/10.1177/2158244015621777

47. Schaeffer, K. (2022, April 25). *In CDC survey, 37% of U.S. high school students report regular mental health struggles during COVID-19 pandemic*. Pew Research Center. https://www.pewresearch.org/fact-tank/2022/04/25/in-cdc-survey-37-of-u-s-high-school-students-report-regular-mental-health-struggles-during-covid-19/

48. McClain, C., Vogels, E. A., Perrin, A., Sechopoulos, S., & Rainie, L. (2021, September 1). *The internet and the pandemic*. Pew Research Center: Internet, Science & Tech. https://www.pewresearch.org/internet/2021/09/01/the-internet-and-the-pandemic/

49. Auxier, B., Anderson, M., Perrin, A., & Turner, E. (2020, July 28). *Parenting children in the age of screens*. Pew Research Center: Internet, Science & Tech. https://www.pewresearch.org/internet/2020/07/28/parenting-children-in-the-age-of-screens/

50. *CDC Covid Data tracker*. Centers for Disease Control and Prevention (CDC). (2023, February 23). https://covid.cdc.gov/covid-data-tracker/#datatracker-home

51. *Covid-19 death data and resources - National Vital Statistics System*. Centers for Disease Control and Prevention (CDC). (2023, February 27). https://www.cdc.gov/nchs/nvss/covid-19.htm

52. Wikimedia Foundation. (2023, March 16). *Impact of the COVID-19 pandemic on other health issues*. Wikipedia. https://en.wikipedia.org/wiki/Impact_of_the_COVID-19_pandemic_on_other_health_issues

53. Wikimedia Foundation. (2023, March 11). *Mental health during the COVID-19 pandemic*. Wikipedia. https://en.wikipedia.org/wiki/Mental_health_during_the_COVID-19_pandemic

54. Wikimedia Foundation. (2023, January 21). *Social impact of the COVID-19 pandemic*. Wikipedia. https://en.wikipedia.org/wiki/Social_impact_of_the_COVID-19_pandemic

55. *The Covid Tracking Project*. The COVID Tracking Project. https://covidtracking.com/

56. Wikimedia Foundation. (2022, December 30). *Impact of the COVID-19 pandemic*. Wikipedia. https://en.wikipedia.org/wiki/Impact_of_the_COVID-19_pandemic

57. Wikimedia Foundation. (2023, March 20). *Impact of the COVID-19 pandemic on children*. Wikipedia. https://en.wikipedia.org/wiki/Impact_of_the_COVID-19_pandemic_on_children

58. Wikimedia Foundation. (2023, March 19). *Impact of the COVID-19 pandemic on education in the United States*. Wikipedia. https://en.wikipedia.org/wiki/Impact_of_the_COVID-19_pandemic_on_education_in_the_United_States

59. Wikimedia Foundation. (2023, February 26). *Impact of the COVID-19 pandemic on long-term care facilities*. Wikipedia. https://en.wikipedia.org/wiki/Impact_of_the_COVID-19_pandemic_on_long-term_care_facilities

60. Wikimedia Foundation. (2023, February 19). *Impact of the COVID-19 pandemic on Prisons*. Wikipedia. https://en.wikipedia.org/wiki/Impact_of_the_COVID-19_pandemic_on_prisons

61. Wikimedia Foundation. (2022, August 28). *Impact of the COVID-19 pandemic on people with disabilities*. Wikipedia. https://en.wikipedia.org/wiki/Impact_of_the_COVID-19_pandemic_on_people_with_disabilities

62. Wikimedia Foundation. (2023, March 20). *Racial disparities in the COVID-19 pandemic in the United States*. Wikipedia. https://en.wikipedia.org/wiki/Racial_disparities_in_the_COVID-19_pandemic_in_the_United_States

63. Wikimedia Foundation. (2023, March 11). *Impact of the COVID-19 pandemic on domestic violence*. Wikipedia. https://en.wikipedia.org/wiki/Impact_of_the_COVID-19_pandemic_on_domestic_violence

64. Wikimedia Foundation. (2022, December 4). *Gendered impact of the COVID-19 pandemic*. Wikipedia.

https://en.wikipedia.org/wiki/Gendered_impact_of_the_COVID-19_pandemic

65. Wikimedia Foundation. (2023, January 22). *Impact of the COVID-19 pandemic on the LGBT Community*. Wikipedia. https://en.wikipedia.org/wiki/Impact_of_the_COVID-19_pandemic_on_the_LGBT_community

66. Wikimedia Foundation. (2021, June 26). *File:cumulative confirmed covid-19 deaths, owid.svg*. Wikipedia. https://en.wikipedia.org/wiki/File:Cumulative_confirmed_COVID-19_deaths,_OWID.svg

67. Wikimedia Foundation. (2022, October 22). *Covid-19 pandemic death rates by country*. Wikipedia. https://en.wikipedia.org/wiki/COVID-19_pandemic_death_rates_by_country

68. Wikimedia Foundation. (2023, March 12). *Food security during the COVID-19 pandemic*. Wikipedia. https://en.wikipedia.org/wiki/Food_security_during_the_COVID-19_pandemic

69. Monte, L. M., & Laughlin, L. (2022, April 6). *Effects of 2020 census-based population controls on 2020 income …* Social, Economic & Housing Statistics Division. https://www.census.gov/content/dam/Census/library/working-papers/2022/demo/sehsd-wp2022-14.pdf

70. Wikimedia Foundation. (2023, January 30). *Impact of the COVID-19 pandemic on Healthcare Workers*. Wikipedia. https://en.wikipedia.org/wiki/Impact_of_the_COVID-19_pandemic_on_healthcare_workers

71. Wang, W. (2014, April 18). *On weekends, dads find more time for leisure than moms*. Pew Research Center. https://www.pewresearch.org/fact-tank/2014/04/18/on-weekends-dads-find-more-time-for-leisure-than-moms/

72. *Caregiving in the US*. The National Alliance for Caregiving. (2023). https://www.caregiving.org/research/caregiving-in-the-us/

IMAGE CREDITS

1. https://pixabay.com/photos/a-book-pen-notebook-writing-paper-1502805/

2. https://pixabay.com/photos/time-hour-hourglass-clock-timer-3961758/

3. https://pixabay.com/photos/piano-concert-music-festival-7559294/

4. https://pixabay.com/photos/concert-live-audience-people-crowd-3387324/

5. https://pixabay.com/photos/piano-rose-red-flower-love-571968/

6. https://pixabay.com/photos/room-show-empty-seat-red-theater-4772780/

7. https://pixabay.com/photos/piano-music-instrument-musician-2617007/

8. https://pixabay.com/photos/people-crowd-hands-clapping-party-2607201/ - cover image

9. https://pixabay.com/photos/hobbiton-hobbit-shire-movie-nature-5284518/

10. https://pixabay.com/photos/wheel-wagon-wheel-old-wood-wooden-1897489/

11. Devin Bard

12. https://pixabay.com/photos/barrier-playground-barrier-tape-4967989/

13. https://pixabay.com/photos/broken-screen-smartphone-6137698/

14. https://pixabay.com/photos/hands-soil-plant-environment-5618240/

15. https://pixabay.com/photos/barefoot-kid-people-little-girl-482747/

16. https://pixabay.com/photos/table-paper-creativity-training-3281047/

17. https://pixabay.com/photos/nature-summer-grass-travel-3245401/ - cover image

18. https://pixabay.com/photos/statue-covid19-coronavirus-mask-5040235/

19. https://pixabay.com/photos/belgium-statue-knokke-beach-2628337/

20. https://pixabay.com/photos/thinking-statue-sitting-statue-2472985/

21. https://pixabay.com/photos/statue-corona-covid-19-face-mask-5069478/

22. https://pixabay.com/photos/mother-child-sculpture-figure-589730/ - cover image

23. https://pixabay.com/photos/statue-sculpture-exhibition-2330254/

24. https://pixabay.com/photos/statues-sculpture-oslo-vigeland-2291148/

25. https://pixabay.com/photos/angel-woman-head-face-figure-2899333/

26. https://pixabay.com/photos/statue-woman-sculpture-female-4809615/

27. https://pixabay.com/photos/stone-statue-lovers-stone-statue-1914898/

28. https://pixabay.com/photos/image-statue-girl-to-talk-fence-2417014/

29. https://pixabay.com/photos/figures-sculpture-togetherness-1691182/

30. https://pixabay.com/photos/buddha-statue-pond-sculpture-1177009/

31. https://pixabay.com/photos/video-call-video-conference-zoom-5962733/

32. https://pixabay.com/photos/cat-small-mackerel-mobile-phone-4793062/

33. https://pixabay.com/photos/elephant-african-bush-elephant-463281/

34. https://pixabay.com/photos/elephant-big-five-nature-water-7716453/

35. https://pixabay.com/photos/elephant-african-bush-elephant-254791/

36. https://pixabay.com/photos/flamingos-birds-herd-beak-pen-3649802/

37. https://pixabay.com/photos/pink-flamingo-lake-nakuru-kenya-1484781/

38. https://pixabay.com/photos/flamingo-water-sun-reflection-1638694/

39. https://pixabay.com/photos/flamingo-bird-water-reflection-5522050/

40. https://pixabay.com/photos/flamingos-birds-animals-wading-bird-7464570/

41. https://pixabay.com/photos/flamingos-birds-pink-animals-bird-1335042/

42. https://pixabay.com/photos/cat-red-cat-kitten-cute-fur-dream-4037007/

43. https://pixabay.com/photos/elephant-gazelle-animals-wild-life-4929027/

44. https://pixabay.com/photos/giraffes-lion-etosha-namibia-4624930/

45. https://pixabay.com/photos/africa-namibia-nature-dry-1170179/

46. https://pixabay.com/photos/amimals-lions-africa-predator-1132745/ - cover image

47. https://pixabay.com/photos/cats-feral-feline-animal-outdoor-2009175/

48. https://pixabay.com/photos/cat-small-mackerel-mobile-phone-4793068/

49. https://pixabay.com/photos/animal-cat-feline-pet-sleeping-6889381/

50. https://pixabay.com/photos/daisy-honor-award-chamaedrys-flower-3102512/

51. https://pixabay.com/photos/butterfly-flowers-pollinate-6527322/

52. https://pixabay.com/photos/daisy-frost-cold-ice-cream-2195525/

53. https://pixabay.com/photos/bee-insect-flower-honey-bee-5618012/

54. https://pixabay.com/photos/flower-meadow-flower-nature-summer-5108121/

55. https://pixabay.com/photos/poppy-field-meadow-flower-grass-3108057/

56. https://pixabay.com/photos/flower-meadow-wildflowers-flower-1491706/

57. https://pixabay.com/photos/flower-meadow-blossoms-4784102/

58. https://pixabay.com/photos/flowers-meadow-nature-wildflowers-3598555/

59. https://pixabay.com/photos/monarch-butterfly-flower-pollinate-5815502/ - cover image

60. https://pixabay.com/photos/bee-insect-flower-honey-bee-animal-170551/

61. https://pixabay.com/photos/bee-peach-blossoms-insect-bumblebee-7299967/

62. https://pixabay.com/photos/butterfly-monarch-insect-wings-bug-18313/

63. https://pixabay.com/photos/lavender-flowers-field-sunrise-6398415/ - cover image

www.ingramcontent.com/pod-product-compliance
Lightning Source LLC
Chambersburg PA
CBHW081935120726
47997CB00010B/3143